A WORLD OF DIFFERENCE

Scotland

Edited by Nina Woodcock

First published in Great Britain in 2008 by:
Young Writers
Remus House
Coltsfoot Drive
Woodston
Peterborough
PE2 9JX
Telephone: 01733 890066
Website: www.youngwriters.co.uk

SB ISBN 978-1 84431 792 9

Foreword

Young Writers' Big Green Poetry Machine is a showcase for our nation's most brilliant young poets to share their thoughts, hopes and fears for the planet they call home.

Young Writers was established in 1990 to nurture creativity in our children and young adults, to give them an interest in poetry and an outlet to express themselves. Seeing their work in print will encourage them to keep writing as they grow, and become our poets of tomorrow.

Selecting the poems has been challenging and immensely rewarding. The effort and imagination invested by these young writers makes their poems a pleasure to enjoy reading time and time again.

Contents

Sophie MacPherson (12)   38
Courtney Beggan (12)   39

Cathkin High School, Cambuslang
Cheryl Lindsay (13)   39
Jamie Loomes (12)   40
Adam Cochrane (13)   40
Fraser Herriot (13)   41
Scott Dobbie (12)   41
Rebecca Ross (12)   42
Warren Morrison (12)   42
Sarah McCleery (13)   43
David Buchanan (12)   43
Fraser Miller (12)   44
Sarah Coyle (13)   44
Eilidh McEwen (12)   45
Kathryn Wilson (13)   45

Clydebank High School, Clydebank
Alexander Gordon (12)   46

Firpark School, Motherwell
Andrew Gray (13)   46

Forfar Academy, Forfar
Oriana Moschovakis (13)   47
Mairi Fugaccia (13)   47

Grantown Grammar School, Moray
Sophie Ramos (16)   48

Kelso High School, Kelso
Zoe Young (12)   48
Mark Tait (12)   49
Greg Davidson (12)   49
Kate Lesenger (12)   50
Delli Woodhead (13)   51
Amelia King (12)   52
Hannah Girrity (14)   53
Rachael Horsburgh (12)   53

Mark McCarry (12)	54
Sophie Douglas (12)	54
Melissa Dunkley (12)	55
Matthew Innes (13)	55
Kyla Hogg (13)	56
Molly Hogg (12)	56
Oran MacKechnie (12)	57
Matt Laidler (12)	57
Zoe Reid (12)	58
Duncan Rennie (13)	58
Gillian Forsyth (14)	59
Ellie Bennett (13)	59
Emma Younger (13)	60
Ryan Paterson (12)	60
Ewan Travers (14)	61
Josh Osbourne (13)	61
Keith Fingland (13)	62
Beth Hadshar (12)	62
Cameron Smith (12)	63
Erin Hastie (13)	63
Ian Peter Reed (13)	64
Cecily Withall (12)	64
Sarah Gibson (15)	65
Michael Berrett (12)	65
Rory Connochie (12)	66
Eilidh Mathewson (12)	66
Levi Hill (12)	67
Kyle David Walker (12)	67
Benjamin Hawkin (12)	68
Aynsley Douglas (12)	68
Rachel Macvicar (13)	69
Cameron Bryce (12)	69
Megan Cuthers (14)	70
Lucy Pringle (12)	70
Daniella Pannone (14)	71
Brittany Barnes (12)	71
Heather Georgina Portsmouth (15)	72
Kirsty Hill (15)	72
Ieeke Green-Roberts (12)	73
Rachael Deans (14)	73
Apithanny Bourne (14)	74
Patricia Fingland (14)	75

Chelsea Blyth (13)	76
Lucy Harding (14)	77
Craig Andrew Riddell (13)	78
Liam Elliot (12)	78
Stacey MacPherson (13)	79
Bruce Easton (13)	79
Kelly Younger (14)	80
Graham Pike (12)	80
Amy Dodds (14)	81
Charlotte Gray (12)	81
Rose Hadshar (14)	82
James Stewart (14)	82
Olivia Robson (14)	83
Marcus Wilson (13)	83
Sophie Fenwick (12)	84
Rachael Bennett (14)	84
Briony Finlayson (12)	85
Liam Hill (13)	85
Abbie Hook (12)	86
Holly Lowrie (13)	86
Natasha Gray (15)	86
Jack Bayram (13)	87
Tessa Hunter (12)	87
Rebecca Rogers (12)	88
Emma Dunkley (12)	88
Rebecca Mark (12)	89

Kilchuimen Academy, Fort Augustus

Shaun Sloggie (13)	89
Tessa Campbell (12)	90
David Saunders (12)	90
Ella Lumsden (13)	91

Kinlochbervie High School, Kinlochbervie

Jaclyn Emma Ross (13)	91
Sophie MacLeod (12)	92
Ruairidh Forbes (13)	92
Erin Kish (12)	93
Eilidh Clark (12)	93
Tom Robbins (12)	94
Mathew James Lenny Hathaway (12)	94

Gary Morrison (13)   94
Elizabeth Marsham (12)   95

Largs Academy, Largs
Charlie Craig (15)   95
Stuart Rintoul (14)   96
Ewen Brennan (15)   96
Jenna Kirk (14)   97
Claire Lennox (15)   97
Laura Bonn (13)   98
Hannah Burns (14)   98
Ruth McClelland (14)   99
Katy Johnstone (14)   99
Sam Hawker (13)   100
Adam Murdoch (14)   100
Lewis Smith (15)   101
William Seaton (15)   101
Katy Raeside (15)   102
Faye Hynds (14)   103
Lewis Thomson (13)   103
Fiona A Clements (14)   104
Katherine Leigh Neilson (14)   105
Sarah Jackson (14)   105
Angela Flack (14)   106
Geraldine Murphy (14)   107
Jennifer Miller (14)   107
Euan Soutter (14)   108

Lornshill Academy, Alloa
Connor Thomson (12)   108
Louise Hall (12)   109
Fiona Gillies (13)   110

Marr College, Troon
Aneesa Burnside McCarthy (12)   110
Callie Dorward (12)   111
Cameron Irvine (12)   111
Joanne Hannah (12)   112
Siobhan Rose (13)   112
Liam Whitten (12)   113
Cieron McDonald (12)   113

Nikki Smyth (13)   114
Louise Martin (12)   114
Matthew Reekie (12)   114
Chloe Dempster (12)   115

Moffat Academy, Moffat
Nicola Henderson (15)   115

St Andrew's RC School, Kirkaldy
Connor Brown   116

St Leonard's School, St Andrews
Imogen Samuel (8)   117

St Modan's High School, Stirling
On Kei Leong (14)   117
Fraser McNair (13)   118
Ross Cunningham (13)   118
Stephen Lewis & Andrew MacDonald (13)   119
Erin Hamill (13)   119
Gemma Miller (13)   119
Emma McCormack (13)   120

Stonelaw High School, Rutherglen
Lesley Wynne (14)   120
Paul Kerr (13)   120
Kate Fell (13)   121
Jessica Richardson (13)   121

Strathallan School, Forgandenny
Gareth Watt (12)   121
Rosie Williams (11)   122
Robyn Somerville (11)   122
Monty Peeters (11)   122

Waid Academy, Anstruther
Blair Watson (12)   123
Lisa Allan (12)   124

The Poems

The Old Man Of The Forest

I stand up tall, rooted to the ground,
My legs don't move, they're ivy bound.
I watch the seasons come and go,
From the Mad March Hare to the winter snow.

My arms, so crooked, so twisted,
Upwards they are lifted,
And then comes my day of dread,
When they chop off my feet and head.

My hair rots away,
I start to decay,
Why did this happen? How can it be?
My life's at an end, it's over for me.

Fraser Dunsmuir (14)

Polar Bear

This world is full of pollution,
Animals near extinction,
Like the mighty polar bear.
His home is being destroyed,
But there are ways we can help him,
By recycling old paper to save a tree limb.

Recycling old cans,
Can help with industry's demands.
Cycle or walk instead of taking the car.
Save the ice caps, don't mar,
Home for endangered polar creatures.
So add a smile to all our features.

Sarah Hector (13)
Aboyne Academy, Aboyne

Climate Change

Ice caps melting,
Temperature changing,
Ozone layer disappearing,
The whole world is changing.

Ice caps melting,
Polar bears dying,
We are all failing,
While global warming's succeeding.

Kirsty Mutch (12)
Aboyne Academy, Aboyne

Recycle

Recycle, recycle,
Green, clear bottles and paper.
Recycle, recycle,
Because the world is dying.
Please recycle to prevent the polar bears crying.

The world is dying of litter,
Please reduce, reuse and recycle.

Kimberley Beveridge (12)
Aboyne Academy, Aboyne

All Alone

I am all alone, sitting on the street,
No comfort, no love,
No water or fresh meat,
I get little money,
Given by passers-by each week!
I'm homeless.

Jodie Shepherd (12)
Aboyne Academy, Aboyne

Fun, Fun, Fun

Recycling is so much fun,
Especially in the sun.
Plastic, glass cans,
All these things can be recycled.

Everyone should recycle
And do more recycling.
It will be so much fun
If you run
And recycle.

Kieron Henderson (13)
Aboyne Academy, Aboyne

Cutting Down The Rainforests

We keep cutting down the rainforests,
The animals and the trees,
We keep cutting down the rainforests,
So it's fine for you and me.
We keep cutting down the oxygen
That we breathe in every day,
We're cutting down the medicine,
Is that really okay?

Elsa Brotchie (12)
Aboyne Academy, Aboyne

Poverty

People who have no choices -
Well, what can I say?
People have to walk miles and miles
To their nearest water supply.
Why must they suffer when we do not?
We do fund raising, but not all the money gets there.
People are dying and nobody is trying,
When we could be flying and supplying.

Charles McIntosh (12)
Aboyne Academy, Aboyne

Pollution

Everywhere in the world
There is pollution.
But for it all there is a simple solution.
Do not litter, make life better
And make the Earth much happier.

Recycle, reuse, give those orders,
Because pollution knows no borders.
Save the Earth, cycle a bit,
Because the Earth really needs it.

All the trees, getting felled
And the rivers getting filled.
Shut down the industries,
Open your mind,
There's a world of possibilities
For you to find.

Joe Whyte (12)
Aboyne Academy, Aboyne

Recycling Is Such A Brilliant Idea

Recycling Is such a brilliant idea,
Everyone should do it.
Cans, glass and plastic bottles,
There isn't that much to it.

Recycling is such a brilliant idea,
Why don't we do it more?
If we try our very best,
Our carbon footprint will be lower.

Recycling is such a brilliant idea,
In order to stop pollution.
If we put our heads together,
We'll find the best solution.

Elizabeth Grace Hazley (12)
Aboyne Academy, Aboyne

No Solution To Pollution

The world is dying,
No one's trying
Ice caps melting,
Rivers drying.

Broken bottles everywhere,
Piles of litter,
No one cares.

Dying trees and bumblebees,
Dead leaves,
Tangled weeds.

The sky will soon be filled with smoke,
The whole planet is starting to choke.
So if we do not start today
To save the planet in any way,
We'll be left with no clue,
With nothing at all that we can do!

Jack Nesbit (12)
Aboyne Academy, Aboyne

Crying In The Night

My name is Darlene,
I am aged thirteen.
I can't sleep in a bed
And my family are all dead.
I need some food and water,
Care, love and laughter.
I need some people in my life,
To stop me crying in the night.
I don't have a home or money,
Any food looks yummy.
My eyes are full of dirt
And my legs really hurt.
Will someone help please, oh please,
Or I will fall down on my knees.

Coralie Dee Arthur (13)
Aboyne Academy, Aboyne

Litter

I hate seeing litter
It is ever so bitter
All over the streets
All over the town
It really makes me frown

Animals can die
Birds won't be able to fly
If they are caught up in it
It's so horrible to think they'll be gone
Just because of litter

I'm going to do something
For towns everywhere
To try and get people to listen
And, hopefully, start to care.

Claire Elizabeth Mathie (13)
Aboyne Academy, Aboyne

Haikus

Tiger
Huge paws pad softly,
through Siberia they roam,
endangered they are.

Snake
Looks wet but is dry,
has no limbs and cannot fly,
climbs trees very high.

Rainforest
Thousands of acres,
natural wonders destroyed,
we need to stop this.

Donald Redpath (13)
Aboyne Academy, Aboyne

Haikus

Poverty
Homeless and starving.
Children hurt, hear them crying.
We must stop this now.

Climate change
Climate change is here.
The world is getting hotter.
We need to act now!

Litter
Litter on the ground,
Lying all around the streets,
Put me in a bin.

Global warming
I have many holes.
I am the ozone layer.
Stop destroying me.

Catriona Swindells (13)
Aboyne Academy, Aboyne

Haikus

Rainforest
Destroying our home.
Save the animals and bugs,
They will have no food.

Don't chop down our home,
I am hungry, I need food,
Please try and help us.

Litter
Don't damage the world,
Keep your rubbish to yourself,
Don't litter your street.

Ione Paterson (12)
Aboyne Academy, Aboyne

Haikus

Summer
Lots of animals
The sun is shining brightly
It's time to sunbathe.

Rainforest
Lots of nice weather
The rainforest is massive
There are animals.

Climate change
The ice is melting
The weather is hot or cold
It's very scary.

Poverty
People are dying
They have no water or food
They are all homeless.

Karen Diane Johnstone (12)
Aboyne Academy, Aboyne

Haiku Poems

Green, green, all around
So please, please, keep it this way
And you'll get your say.

Traffic moving slow
Releasing fumes as it goes.
Ice caps melting, *no!*

Winter's coming fast,
The snow will cover the grass.
It will soon be past.

Lewis Smith (12)
Aboyne Academy, Aboyne

Haikus

Recycling
Don't drop your litter
Reduce, reuse, recycle
Make the world better.

Climate change
The world is heating
Ice caps melting all the time
Help us to save the world.

Poverty
People on the streets
They are poor and are hungry
They are cold and sad.

Rainforests
Homes for many tribes
Trees are as high as the sky
Animals love it.

Pollution
Oil spills and car fumes
Are destroying all the world
It's changing our lives.

Sian Fish (12)
Aboyne Academy, Aboyne

Recycling - Haikus

Reduce your rubbish
Reuse your old glass bottles
Recycle paper.

Keep the world tidy
Reuse paper and plastic
Recycle all waste.

Megan Donaldson (12)
Aboyne Academy, Aboyne

Haiku Poems

Climate change
All of the car fumes
Make ozone layer go brown
Drivers please don't zoom.

Paper wasting
Please don't waste paper
You're making the trees get chopped
Please, please, stop right now.

Summer
Sun shining so bright
People playing in the park
Summer is now here.

Cameron Giblin (12)
Aboyne Academy, Aboyne

Haikus

Rainforests
Monkeys swing from trees.
Sun then rain, now lightning comes.
Natives gather food.

Poverty
Kids huddled in streets.
Hungry for food and water.
Change rattling in pots.

Pollution
Cities full of fumes.
Vehicles turn air to smog.
Countryside, fresh air.

Kirsty Mackenzie (12)
Aboyne Academy, Aboyne

Problems

Litter makes life worse
In ways I can't explain.
If only we weren't bitter
We could take the blame.

Pollution is crazy
With rubbish that's a tip,
If only we weren't lazy
We'd tidy up a bit.

The rainforests are going,
It's very near,
They might stop growing
Or even disappear.

The ice caps are shrinking,
The polar bears are dying.
This will need some thinking,
Really, we're not lying.

Daniel Fraser (13)
Aboyne Academy, Aboyne

Haikus

So hot, so humid.
People swimming in the sea.
Do you wish you did?

Lotion gets sprayed on.
No one wanting to get burnt.
People sunbathing.

Watch out for poachers.
They are so deadly to you.
Animals beware.

Craig Stephen (12)
Aboyne Academy, Aboyne

The Disappearing Forests

Rainforests are only a flight away,
Well, that's what we say.
Being destroyed day by day,
Where will the animals stay?

Millions of plants, animals and insects live there today,
How many will survive until tomorrow?
All the plants, animals and trees,
They need your help, please.

Climate change and heat rising,
Heavy rainstorms fall more and more,
From high above the trees are falling,
The canopy protects no more.

Erin Bell (12)
Ayr Academy, Ayr

Children's Plea

Before you go and wreck our world,
We children ask that we be heard,
We wish to live with no stress,
Instead of cleaning up your mess.
We will be blamed for your destruction,
All because you took no action.
It's not too late to stop this cycle,
Think of your child and then recycle.
Bottles, paper, cans and tins,
Stop our world from caving in.
This is one child's final plea -
Do not take my world from me.

Karen Geddes (13)
Banchory Academy, Banchory

Help The World

Stop dropping litter,
The world's getting bitter,
Soon icebergs are going to melt.

Stop using your car,
You can cycle quite far,
Soon icebergs are going to melt.

Start recycling more,
It's not a chore,
Soon icebergs are going to melt.

The planet's in a mess,
Start using less,
Soon icebergs are going to melt.

The world's going to die,
Time to say goodbye,
'Cause icebergs are going to melt.

Katie Cousland (12)
Banchory Academy, Banchory

Green

Don't drop your litter,
do as we say,
chuck it in the bin
and you will make our day.
if there is not a bin,
put it in your pocket,
if you do this
you will help save the environment,
if you don't do this,
the world will fall into turmoil.

Jamie Mackie (12) & Michael Cobban (13)
Banchory Academy, Banchory

Go Green

Use a bike, or even walk,
It's even better than driving.
Cut down on your carbon emissions
And get the Arctic thriving.

We must save electricity,
Every single year.,
To stop the ice caps melting,
Then we can give a cheer.

Reduce, reuse, recycle,
That's what everyone says,
But if we decide to cycle to work
We may get a few more days.

Because the planet is slowly dying,
And soon we may have to leave,
Prevent the animals from frying,
So we don't have to grieve.

Alasdair McCrone (12)
Banchory Academy, Banchory

Green Poem

E nvironmentally friendly.
N ever drop litter.
V anish plastic bags.
I ce is melting in the Arctic
R ecklessness of humans.
O zone layer breaking.
N o Fossil Fuels
M urdering Mother Earth.
E arth is dying.
N ight is ruined, no more stars.
T omorrow may never come.

Jack Fraser (12)
Banchory Academy, Banchory

Big, Green Poem

The planet's in a mess,
We've got to use less.

Don't drop any litter,
Or it will make the world bitter.

Cycling more and driving less,
Helps to prevent the planet's stress.

Please don't take the car,
If it's really not too far.

Switch off your bedroom light
And go outside and fly your kite.

Turn off your telly
And stop stuffing your belly.

Please remember to recycle
And start to use your bicycle.

The planet's in a mess,
We've got to use less.

Catherine Thomson & Annie Ross (12)
Banchory Academy, Banchory

Trees

Trees are destroyed, we need to stop.
All of them are about to drop.
We can't help it, that's our excuse,
But the trees are getting much abuse.

We all can stop by using bins
And recycling all of those tins.
Don't you think we are being so cruel?
A tree might even land on a poor mule.

Daniel Fitzgerald (13)
Banchory Academy, Banchory

The Path To A Greener World

What is wrong with the world?
Everything is such a mess.
Recycle more,
Throw out less,
Make the world a happy place.

Stop cutting down trees,
Animals will be extinct,
So save the chimpanzees.
Greenhouse gases disappear,
Make the world a happy place.

Just by dropping litter
Makes everything bitter.
Ruining the ozone isn't very far,
Make the world a happy place.

Everything is getting hotter,
It was just so easy to solve,
Everyone work together,
We're going to save the world!

An age when there are no cars,
To ruin everything that's been done,
So keep on looking forward,
We've saved the world.

Sarah Baker (13)
Banchory Academy, Banchory

Altogether Now

It's fair for God to judge us,
For the awful things we've done,
Pollution, greenhouse, CO_2,
This means nought to some.
But to others it consumes them,
For they care about their home,
Recycle, reuse, cutting down,
They shouldn't have to do alone.

Emily Sansom (13)
Banchory Academy, Banchory

Help The Homeless

There he sat with half a cup,
Begging for change to set him up.
He sat in the alleyway without a friend,
He wondered when this nightmare would end.
The man used the money for even more drink,
The further down his life would sink.
There he slept under a bin,
People walked by, saying, 'That's a sin.'

As the years went on the man got thinner,
He was begging for money for his dinner.
He became filthy on the outside
But even more bitter on the inside.
They can't do it themselves, they need someone to lead,
Please help the homeless, they're in desperate need.

John Ingram (12) & Blair Sharkie (13)
Bellshill Academy, Bellshill

Goodbye Rainforest

R aindrops dripping on green leaves,
A nimals running around the foot of the trees.
I cky, sticky bugs live in the mud,
N ature has fallen with a thud.
F orests have been here so long.
O ur nature has now all gone wrong.
R oads being built through the green grass,
E ach day life gets low class.
S o help us keep our forest safe,
T o make our Earth a better place.

Ainsley Roe (14), Philip Norton & Lisa Findlay
Bellshill Academy, Bellshill

End This Torture

Help the homeless, they have nowhere to stay.
'Any spare change,' that's what they always say.
They live in the bins or in the street,
Searching but finding nothing to eat.
They wander around, they begin to roam,
They're searching the streets for a brand new home.
They try and try, but never succeed,
They can't do it themselves, they need someone to lead.
They are only human, they need a house,
They shouldn't need to roam the street like a mouse.
They are covered in mud, but they don't have a shower,
They need to stand up for themselves and take more power.
Give up the jokes if you know how,
End this torture, stop it *now!*

Gemma Bissett, Lynsay O'Donohue (12) & Kelly Pratt (13)
Bellshill Academy, Bellshill

Litter

L eft on our streets, pavements and drains
I t's thrown out of our cars and trains
T ons and tons of litter left each day
T housands more about to be thrown away
E nvironment wants a cleaner town
R ecycle your litter and don't throw it down.

L andfill sites are not very nice
I know they attract birds, rats and mice
T hese places are full of disease
T etanus is one if you scratch your knees
E nd careless dumping at home and on the street
R ubbish is all it takes to stop a heartbeat.

Sophie North (13), Kirsten Liddell & Andrew Baxter
Bellshill Academy, Bellshill

Slaughter On The Ice

The heartless hunter, with a long, solid baseball bat,
Stands over the innocent seals and bashes their heads.
Helpless, adorable babies crying out loud.
Navels getting slit, up to their chins,
Little naked, bleeding bodies piled upon the ice.
We will catch this killer, you and I.

The warm-hearted Eskimo was killing for survival,
Hunting from a kayak, keeping very quiet,
The skin he wore to keep him warm,
His bow and arrow shaped at the ready,
Getting meat to provide for his family.

Capes, coats, gloves and boots,
All promoted in fashion magazines.
Souvenirs and postcards,
Showing a trail of naked carcasses.
Shall we take this callous killer
And dispose of him together?

The only way to do it is to shun,
The seal skin product.
Maybe, next year, we can face the spring together,
With a picture free of cold-blooded seal killing and misery.
We can stop this, yes we can,
We will do it, you and I.

Ailsa Reid (12)
Breadalbane Academy, Aberfeldy

Blood Of A Bull

The arena was surrounded by a thousand people,
Tightly packed in tiers,
Many of them waving programmes in front of their faces,
Trying to shift the sluggish air.
Although we were seated,
None were still.
A small, brass band playing in the far corner,
They were wearing neat, military uniforms,
Like little toy soldiers.
A small, green tractor drove towards the gate,
Dragging behind it a large, black lump that had,
Until seconds ago, been a proud, living being.
Dozens of brightly coloured spears dangled out of the creatures back
And as it drew nearer the glistening red line in the sand grew longer.
The smell of blood and animal sweat riveted the screaming fans,
But as the trumpet sounded the next fight
The cheer only grew louder.
A man in an elaborate suit of sequins, colour and silk
Strutted out into the middle of the arena,
Arrogant and proud,
Awaiting his glorious prey.
Another gate was opened
And the mighty mass of muscle thundered into the ring,
Like a bullet from a gun.
Right now he was ignoring the matador,
Running madly in a jagged circle,
Kicking out his back legs,
Enraged by the lights and the shouting fans.
Then the bull noticed him.
The crowd fell silent as it lumbered towards him,
Coming to a halt about twenty metres away,
Its head low, its horns pointing at the target.
The bull charged,
Its massive shoulders heaving,
Its every muscle concentrated on the man that stood ahead.
But the matador was too quick.
He summoned great speed, diving under the bull
And grabbing the banderilla spear at the same time.
The attack was fierce and brutal.

Young Writers - A World Of Difference Scotland

The long, barbed hook was plunged deep into the creature's neck
And as it struggled to pull it out
More and more were jolted in.
Twelve of the banderilla spears hung from the creature.
The bull staggered mercifully towards the great hero,
The sadness was deep in its eyes,
But with a jolt of his arm
The matador struck the weakness to the floor.
The mighty beast lay in the sand,
And so it would remain,
Until the trumpets sounded again.

Brandon Evans (13)
Breadalbane Academy, Aberfeldy

Born To Be Eaten

Spring
The best days of the year,
Bluebells, daisies, blue skies and sun!
A new beginning! Daffodils, blossom, new leaves,
Lambs.

Lambs
Clouds with legs,
Frolicky, bouncy, cuddly, cute,
Picture it!
Bleating, baaing, grazing and lazing!

Lambs
Crammed in lorries,
Stressed, messed, waiting, waiting.
Cuddly and cute no more,
Lying in a heap by the door!

Lambs,
Meat on plates!

Harriet Lawson (12)
Breadalbane Academy, Aberfeldy

Animal Testing

I guess it's perfectly usual,
There are lots of animals here,
At least I have got a home,
But they put shampoo in my ear.

Hopefully I am being useful,
For the products I test,
The animals here aren't so friendly,
I guess I'm just a pest.

They put liquid in my eyes,
That makes me weep with no surprise.
I wish they would stop doing this,
It confuses me inside.

I do go through a lot of pain,
But it is for something good.
I suffer as they stick needles into me,
But it is for something very good.

The question is, what are they trying to do?
It's probably something really important,
Why else would they do it?
I guess it's perfectly usual, I'm not the only one here.

I guess this is what animals are meant for,
There is nothing else for me!
Stuck in a laboratory for the rest of my life,
Oh how I wish I could be free.

Fiona Logan (13)
Breadalbane Academy, Aberfeldy

Elephants

Elephants in the wild,
Elephants in the zoo,
Elephants should be protected,
Not shot by you.

Help us, oh help us,
Before they become extinct.
Help us, oh help us,
Before they become extinct.

Poaching is really disgusting,
I hate it, so should you.
You make them walk into sharp, pointed traps
And make them suffer for ornaments, just for you.

Help us, oh help us,
Before they become extinct.
Help us, oh help us,
Before they become extinct.

Elephants are as big as houses,
They're big, grey, beautiful creatures.
But you seem to hate them and kill,
So you can play their tusks on a big, brown piano.

Help us, oh help us,
Before they become extinct.
Help us, oh help us,
Before they become extinct.

Ivory is made from tusks,
Believe me this is true.
Phone covers, jewellery, even piano keys,
These elephants die for you.

Alice Thompson (12)
Breadalbane Academy, Aberfeldy

I Am A Tiger

I am a tiger
Hunting for my prey,
The deer are all about
In the middle of the day.

I am a tiger
Camouflaged by the tree,
The poachers are hunting
But they can't see me.

I am a tiger
Look at me today,
As for later on,
Well, what can I say?

I am a tiger
They've left me so blue,
Day after day I watch
In case they come too.

I am a tiger
Look at me now,
No fur, stuffed,
You should see me now!

I am a tiger,
Nearly extinct,
Please help us,
We'll be lost in a blink.

I am a *tiger!*

Shannon Melvin (12)
Breadalbane Academy, Aberfeldy

What Am I?

You cut me down,
You take me away,
You put me together
And sell me for pay.

What am I?

I'm homeless, alone,
No shelter, no home,
Dirty water, no food,
No hope but you.

What am I?

I'm slaughtered
I'm used for you,
You use me for meat,
My insides for medicine, my fur for clothes.

What am I?

You pollute my air,
You put oil in my seas,
You kill a lot of animals
And who does it please?

What am I?

I cut down rainforests,
I don't help the less fortunate,
I am cruel to animals
And I pollute my planet.

What am I?

You!

Freya Broad (13)
Breadalbane Academy, Aberfeldy

It Was A Sell Out

I stood there, staring
Just over there beside that tiny arena.
I felt like an idiot - standing and staring.
How could they stand, laugh and cheer?

Those big cockerels, what did they do wrong?
I felt like an idiot - standing and staring.
They were jumping and hissing like snakes.
All that palaver for nothing.

One threw itself at its opponent, like a flying squirrel.
The other dodged it and made its move,
It closed its beak, hard, on the others wing
Before it screeched like a hyena.
Then a kick.

An attempt at death, I think it was,
For those people's pleasure.
I felt like an idiot - standing and staring,
The cheering stopped as one fell to the ground
- but didn't die.

The fight was over, thank goodness for that.
There was a loud gunshot, I jumped to the left.
I felt like an idiot - standing and staring.
Both cockerels were dead.

Lorna McLachlan (12)
Breadalbane Academy, Aberfeldy

Left Alone

I've wagged my tail and I've licked your hand,
I came to your call and every demand.
I gave you my trust and my heart too,
I sat in the yard and watched over you.
I love you, that is why for your attention I plead,
I was hurt really bad when you made me bleed.
I run to your presence when you are near,
Yet you betrayed me, struck me with fear.
I lay on the ground, my fur full of dirt,
With an empty bowl, as my stomach hurt.
My mouth grew dry when my water was gone,
I could feel myself sick, it would last for so long.
I wait and I wait for a bite to eat,
A droplet of water, or a tasty treat.
You have left me and I don't know why,
I was your loyal companion, I stayed by your side.
The days are growing long and I feel really sad,
I feel all alone and my health is so bad.
I lie here from weakness, unable to stand,
I still feel so lonely, I just need a hand.

Kyle Allen (12)
Breadalbane Academy, Aberfeldy

Just For Fun

Life for me was very fine,
Now all I do is sit and pine
For all the bears I left behind,
Why can't life just rewind?

They sat me on a wooden chair,
Then what they did was just not fair,
They took out all my nails and teeth,
Then left me whining in my grief.

Following the needle there was a rope,
All I could do was hope and hope.
The pain I felt was just atrocious,
It really left me feeling nauseous.

Next thing I knew I was on the street,
With fire burning round my feet.
They laughed at me and teased me,
Took pictures and uneased me.

I know I'm not the only one,
There's others suffering, just for fun.

Corrie Allan (13)
Breadalbane Academy, Aberfeldy

Pollution Poem

Pollution, what a terrible thing.
Pollution makes the world sing
For a solution to stop pollution.
Pollution needs to be minimised.
The people around the world should open
Their eyes and see what they are doing.
Don't wait for it to get worse,
The ozone is about to burst!

Brooke Graham (12)
Buckhaven High School, Fife

Eco Poem

Please don't throw away
Your litter today.
Please do your best
To fix our mess
That we've created
By being careless.

Don't say I'll leave it
For another day,
The time to act is right away!
So please act now before it's too late
To save our planet from decay.

Our rainforests are getting cut down,
Recycle paper and don't be a clown!

Global warming is no longer a threat,
It's here to stay, but do not fret.
We can still slow it down
If we all do our bit
Around our town.

Harry Cairns (12)
Buckhaven High School, Fife

Recycling

Hear the bottles as they smash
Into the bin with a clash.
Help recycle and save some cash,
Make them into smart new glass.

Recycling is fun! So do it.

Jodie Pratt (12)
Buckhaven High School, Fife

Make Our World Fit

The horrible, minging pollution
That really needs a solution,
So here are some tips
To make our world fit!

Litter is rather bitter,
So recycle the paper after your fritters.

Reuse your carrier bags from Tesco
So you won't be eating alfresco . . .
In December!

Snow through the middle of spring,
Flowers in the winter,
Very sunny through autumn
And dead leaves in the summer.

Global warming is man-made
So I guess
It's nothing to do with women!

Reduce the amount of rubbish
And the world won't slip!

Hannah Smart
Buckhaven High School, Fife

Recycling

If you recycle
You'll be surprised
At the changes you'll notice
Right before your eyes.

You will be helping
The world around you
By reusing objects,
It's easy to do.

Just recycle cardboard,
Cans or paper,
And help make the world
Free from litter caper.

Now you are ready,
1 . . . 2 . . . 3 . . .
Go!
And help make the world litter free.

Liam Cunningham (12)
Buckhaven High School, Fife

The World Of Wounds

The once blue sky is filled with black,
Spitting grime from their chimney stacks.
Monstrous factories making their print,
Polar bears, beautiful, but becoming extinct.

Burns and lakes, oceans and seas,
So natural and calm, have a think please!
Cans and bikes, buckets and bins,
Ruining nature, isn't it a sin?

Your children and mine are the ones who will pay,
What can we do about this today?
Cut down on cars and switch off your lights,
This will make the world, once more, a beautiful sight.

Before there were TVs and cars alike,
The world was such a wonderful sight.
There's so many things that we could do
To change the world, it's up to you!

Sarah Brown (14)
Carrick Academy, Maybole

Trees

I am a tree standing proud
With all the other handsome trees.
I am a helpless tree, standing still
Watching all the innocent trees being cut down.
I am a tree, standing still
Alone now
About to be cut down.
I am a tree, lying on the ground,
Lifeless and dead, but innocent.
There are no trees left now,
Do you really need all that paper?

Shannon McGarrie
Carrick Academy, Maybole

Polar Bear

I'm sitting on a sinking ship,
Soon I will have no choice but to take a dip.
My world is melting,
Acid rain is pelting,
My cubs are dying,
I must keep trying
To keep myself alive.

Do you know all about my worries?
The rest of my kind are all in flurries
About the melting ice.
But all my cubs are dying out,
It just makes me want to shout.
Why can't you just think of us?
Why isn't everyone making a fuss?
We live in this world too,
But real soon it will just be you!

Louise Martin (13)
Carrick Academy, Maybole

Save Us

Creatures of the Earth are in danger,
The polar bears' ice palace is melting,
The tigers' rainforest is deserting,
The elephants are disappearing.
While we should be pioneering in every way we can,
To protect these creatures and their land.

Whales are hunted,
Man is minted,
Dolphins are caught in nets,
Baby alligators are kept as pets.
So we should be pioneering in every way we can,
To protect these creatures and their land.

Katie Forson (12)
Carrick Academy, Maybole

Withering Away

My leaves are gone
I'm all alone
You didn't care
And now I'm bare
I needed help when I was weak
You climbed up me but I couldn't speak
I'm withering away
Pollution made it this way
My roots are dead
My leaves shed
You could have helped
But you ran away
Yes, I'm a tree
But soon won't be.

Jodie Wallace (12)
Carrick Academy, Maybole

The Racism Rap

It's all about black versus white,
Racism is simply just not right,
Blacks are blacks, whites are whites,
Let's just stop all these fights.

All across the nation is hunger and starvation,
All across the nation is racism and discrimination,
All cross this nation is poverty and overpopulation.

Why don't we stop this pain?
There's a lot more we can gain,
Why not help each other
Instead of killing one another?

Actions speak louder than words,
So let's do something about it!
Whether I am black or white,
I am feeling it ma bruvvah!

Adam Copeland (12)
Carrick Academy, Maybole

Waste

Our world is warming up
The ice is slowly melting
Polar bears dying out
Trees falling down
Homeless animals suffering
Smoke affects the air
No more fresh air
No more trees to
Sway in the breeze
Throwing litter
On the streets
Is dirty and bad
Our world is not a
Waste bin
It's a place that
We live in
So keep it clean and tidy.

Amy Boyd (12)
Carrick Academy, Maybole

Save The World From Poverty

Starving children in poor countries,
Hungry adults with no food or money,
Danger of death, they are all skin and bone,
So why don't we all give Trocaire a phone.

Make poverty history, all in the past,
Give poor people jobs to help them last.
Fading away, hungry, alone,
Why aren't we helping, just a little phone?

Dying of thirst, with no running water,
A man all alone because poverty took his daughter.
No food, no water, soon there'll be nothing,
Come and give poverty fighters a ring.

Joanne Shennan (13)
Carrick Academy, Maybole

World

The world, our home,
With trees that rise
And trees that fall,
They shape the Earth
A view for us all.
We slice them down
Without a thought,
Loggers and litterers
Should be shot.
Animals die
From our mistakes,
No one cares
About the lives we take.
Birds will fall
Out of the sky,
The fish won't bite,
Soon all will die.
The world, our home
Needs renovating,
The windows need polishing
The air needs to be cleaned,
Smoke and pollution
A terrible fiend.

Connar Cluckie (12)
Carrick Academy, Maybole

Hear Our Planet

Many years from now
The world could be covered in ice
Or millions of people could die in the heat
And we still carry on despite.

Why are doing this to our world?
The world that we all live in
The only person who seems to care is me
And yet we still carry on in sin.

Trash has covered our Earth
Our streams are nothing but mud
Where have all the singing birds gone?
I miss them and I also think you should.

The Earth is suffering
The Earth is sad
And yet we all sit and do nothing
As if we are glad.

How long will our planet be able to put up with it?
It's screaming, can't you hear it?
Maybe I'll be the first one to listen
While you stay there and sit.

The cars that we use are monsters
We should only use them if we have to
Get on a public bus
Everyone does it so why shouldn't you.

Let's all put our hands together
And admit that we are wrong
The ones that get up and do something
Well, they are the most strong!

Look after our planet.

Sian Louise Bird (14)
Carrick Academy, Maybole

The Environment

T rees help us breathe
H armful fumes make us heave
E verywhere there is smoke

E verywhere people choke
N ot everyone is taking heed
V ery worrying indeed!
I diots throw their litter away
R eally caring ones have their say
O ne day we will see
N one of this was meant to be
M any things won't look nice
E ven the Arctic's losing ice
N ow we must let the world heal
T oday is the time to feel.

Mark Graham (12)
Carrick Academy, Maybole

Litter

My name is Lin
I am a bin
No one likes me, no one uses me
I am black and also round
Every day I watch people throwing litter on the ground
It blows high in the sky and makes me cry
Cans and bottles, crisp packets too
Chewing gum that sticks to your shoe
Litter's a disgrace, so keep it in place
Now I'm going to tell you one more thing
Put your litter in the bin!

Sophie MacPherson (12)
Carrick Academy, Maybole

War

I don't see the need for all this war
It's just corrupting people
Wrecking homes, making people poor
Chemical burns on blistered babies
Rats feeding on severed limbs, spreading rabies
A mother cries for her son lost among the rubble
It's just like another world
Inside a violent bubble
The price of oil
Is paid in bodies
No hospitals left to care for anybody
As the bombs fall over and round about
The citizens just want to be out of this town.

Courtney Beggan (12)
Carrick Academy, Maybole

Trees, Grass And Plants

The trees are green
The grass is green
Some plants are green
So don't *vandalise* green

Green, green, green, that's all you see,
But now green, green, green, you don't see.

Now there are hardly any trees and grass
We must save the trees and grass, at last!

So now that we are saving the trees
Now recycle paper.
Please, please, please!

Cheryl Lindsay (13)
Cathkin High School, Cambuslang

Warning

Warning, warning
Global warming
Trees are falling
Please help we're falling

Birds are choking on your litter
Pick it up
Or you'll feel so bitter

Your carbon footprint
Is so high
Keep it down
Or we'll all die

Too many fumes
In the air
Walk or cycle
You'll still get there

Please have a heart
Stop polluting
Let's make a fresh start!

Jamie Loomes (12)
Cathkin High School, Cambuslang

War, What Is It Good For?

People cause wars,
Because of silly arguments.
War is good for nobody,
It causes pain and death.
People are dying everywhere.
Bombs blowing,
Guns blazing.
People dying because of war.

Adam Cochrane (13)
Cathkin High School, Cambuslang

Extinction

Animals, animals where are you going?
Is it our acts of stupidity that are driving you to extinction?

Pandas, why are you dying?
Is it us taking your food and habitat?
Is it us that is driving you to extinction?

Tigers, tigers, why are you leaving this world?
Is it poaching you with guns and knives
That is taking your lives?
Is it us that is driving you to extinction?

Turtles, is the ocean that bad?
Are we polluting the water
And killing and skinning you for leather
Is it us that is driving you to extinction?

Animals, animals, is it us that is wiping you out?
Is it our laziness and cowardliness
That is polluting this Earth and destroying your habitats?
Is it us that is driving you to extinction?

Fraser Herriot (13)
Cathkin High School, Cambuslang

What Shall We Do?

Pollution, pollution, what is the solution?
Global warming that is the problem.
Ozone layer, ozone layer, what is the problem up there?
Petrol fumes poisoning the city air.
Indeed, indeed, plant some more seeds,
Trees getting cut down, oxygen is going to waste.
Glass, glass, why do you smash
And ruin the landscape in our countryside?
Pollution, pollution, I know a solution,
Use less transport or stop using fire to get rid of rubbish.

Scott Dobbie (12)
Cathkin High School, Cambuslang

Tree

My granddad took me to the museum today, where I saw the
strangest thing.
It was a big picture in a glass cabinet and the caption read,
'The Tree:
The tree became extinct in 2058 due to deforestation'.
In the rocket I asked Grandad if he remembered the trees.
'I do,' he said,
'They were big, had sturdy, wooden trunks, long branches and
green leaves.'
He sighed, 'They told us, the scientists, they all said,
If you don't stop cutting down the trees there'll be no more.'
He sighed for a second time,
'If only we'd listened, we wouldn't have had to live here.'

We landed on the moon.

Rebecca Ross (12)
Cathkin High School, Cambuslang

Just Think

The litter, the drugs
and the CFCs,
how can something so small
be killing something as big as me?
Vandalism,
Chopping down trees,
Shooting animals,
Why would you want to do this to me?
Killing the animals, making them extinct,
people just think!

Warren Morrison (12)
Cathkin High School, Cambuslang

Play Your Part In This

The Earth, it is a wonderful place, with big, tall trees and flowers, with
scorching, burning desert air and rain that make us wet.
The forest floor covered in leaves, the size of my hand,
But don't be fooled, it's not all like this,
We're the monsters in disguise.

If we love our world so much, why don't we just recycle?
The graffiti on the gates and walls is like us being so small and what
about the atmosphere, with all the super cars?
The pollution in them is so much, but we drive them anyway.

The rainwater goes splish, splash, splosh when it hits the
concrete ground.
The parks are good for sunny days, to run and laugh and shout, and
the soft grass is mostly there to get greener and greener every day, but
our carbon footprint will always be there no matter what we do.

The litter that you throw away and not put in the bins,
Does not disappear just like that, it stays for lots of years.
So when you are very old you'll think back on what I've said, but by
then it won't be real oak trees, it will be *kid on* ones instead.

Sarah McCleery (13)
Cathkin High School, Cambuslang

Goodbye Planet

Why are you doing this?
Please stop, please.
The animals are my friends,
Can't you just leave the environment alone?

The racism is very bad.
Why do people judge others by the colour of their skin?
My friends are different colours and religions.
But I don't care,
They are my friends.

David Buchanan (12)
Cathkin High School, Cambuslang

Car Pollution

C an we help stop car pollution?
A re we making a big mess of the world?
R emember the time the world was all clean?

P eople think it is bad using cars too much.
O ur world is going to die if we don't stop polluting it.
L ittle kids don't notice this is happening.
L ook and see all of the fumes coming out of cars.
U ntidy world, full of fumes and mess.
T idy up this big mess by walking to school or walking to the shops.
I do my bit for the environment by walking to school.
O ver there I see lots of fumes and smog.
N ext time your mum or dad is going to drive you to school, say *no!*

Fraser Miller (12)
Cathkin High School, Cambuslang

Recycling

R is for recycling, that many folk don't do.
E is for the Earth that you are damaging too.
C is for the Coke cans, Irnbru and more, that young people leave
    lying on the floor.
Y is for you, the person who litters,
C Can you stop getting very bitter.
L it's gonna be a long, long time before it's all cleaned up.
I could always recycle a plastic cup
N is for nothing is more cool than recycling.
G is for giving things another chance,
    That is my thing.

Sarah Coyle (13)
Cathkin High School, Cambuslang

Litter

Litter is like a bit of muck
Litterbugs are just like mugs
Litter is a piece of dirt
Litter is a filthy sea of dirt.
Rolling, ripping, rustling the crisp packets goes, it blows.

Litter goes further and further away
The can goes boom, slam, twang, when it hits the ground
The can is angry
The can likes to be in a bin with all its litter friends
The wrapper of the chocolate bar floats really, really far.
I do not like litter.

Eilidh McEwen (12)
Cathkin High School, Cambuslang

Save The Animals

Save the monkeys and chimpanzees
Stop cutting down the trees
Save the tigers and pandas too
It's really all up to you
Save the eagles to stop them frown
Stop the hunter shooting them down
Save the animals, please help
To stop them cry and squeal and yelp.

Kathryn Wilson (13)
Cathkin High School, Cambuslang

The Recycling Poem

Whether it be plastic bottles,
the old, little toys your brother throttles,
used paper, soft drink cans,
useless junk, dusty pans.

Old magazines, cardboard boxes,
don't leave the reusable stuff to the boxes,
sweetie wrappers, all this stuff
don't just leave it to gather fluff.

All the stuff that you can't use,
old notes, last week's news,
stick them in the recycling bin, yes, the lot!
All join in the recycling plot.

Save the world, do it right,
let's all help win the fight,
have a laugh, make it fun,
everyone do the recycling run.

So the next time you see a plastic thing,
please don't just shove it in the bin,
do what's right, listen to what I say,
it's just recycling all the way!

Alexander Gordon (12)
Clydebank High School, Clydebank

Animals

Animals
Rhinos
Tigers
Eating
Sleeping
Roaring
Not killing them for money
Animals.

Andrew Gray (13)
Firpark School, Motherwell

Death

Death. If only I could explain death.
I've been there once, only once.
Been in the blackness of the street,
The gutters of the city.

Death. If only everyone knew how that felt,
Maybe no one would try suicide.
If only they knew their problems wouldn't end.

Death. If only I could say how it kills.
When you are screaming at the lonely silence
And you cannot go back again.

Death. If only everyone knew it,
Then there would be no wars,
No suicides, no murders.
Death.

Oriana Moschovakis (13)
Forfar Academy, Forfar

Help

Trees cut down, forests stripped,
People homeless, on the streets,
Voices screaming, needing help,
Can we help or are we too late?

People starving, eating nothing,
Working hard, getting less money,
Forests flattened, factories made,
Can we help, or are we too late?

People sleeping in the cold,
Many suffering - young and old,
Can we help or are we too late?
We *can* help, it's not too late!

Mairi Fugaccia (13)
Forfar Academy, Forfar

The Nobodies

Another sorrowful expression:
Legs crossed,
Hands out-stretched,
Pity strikes hard.
I sprinkle pennies at their feet,
I'm thanked, with a gracious nod
And a fading smile.
Copper lines their pockets now.
Just another face on a busy street;
A passing thought,
A fading memory.

Sophie Ramos (16)
Grantown Grammar School, Moray

The Cold Continent

Glaciers creak as you listen closely
Lots of snow, ice and air
Big and white
Bright and blue
Penguins, seals and fish

It looks so clear
So fresh and crisp
But it really is under threat
All of our pollution
Can damage it

The smell of salt
The bitter crunch of snow
It all looks so amazing
So cool, so fresh, so breathtaking
We cannot let it go.

Zoe Young (12)
Kelso High School, Kelso

Amazing Antarctica

The coldness in the air,
It makes you shiver
The wind whistles past,
Slipping on the ice.

The pure, blue water,
The different colours in the sunset,
The white ice underneath you,
Everywhere you look, you see white.

The fresh air all around you,
The taste of sea salts in your mouth,
Looking across an empty landscape.

Finding new discoveries,
Sending the ROV deep underneath the water,
Divers diving below the thick ice,
Finding new medicines.

Mark Tait (12)
Kelso High School, Kelso

Antarctica

A rched shapes lie on the ground
N o dust or sand, just lying snow
T reading through the snow, step by step
A lot of snow
R estless scientists working all night
C rack of breaking ice
T iny penguins sliding on the ice
I cebergs standing tall
C hubby penguins, like men in dinner suits
A round the South Pole snow falls.

Greg Davidson (12)
Kelso High School, Kelso

Antarctica

Antarctica, a continent surrounded by oceans,
In the Southern Hemisphere,
as far away from the Equator as you can get.
Centred on the South Pole, no wonder it's so cold.

With it's permanent ice sheet covering the land
And icebergs and ice shelves and glaciers, you can tell,
Surprisingly, animals and plants live there as well.
Seals moan and groan, but that's how they talk
And penguins squawk 24/7, around the clock.
Plants live and grow, sometimes under the snow,
But let's get on with Antarctica, you know.

There are the sharp beaks of the penguins
And round bodies of seals
And the gliding, narrow wings of the albatross,
Make them as beautiful to watch as eagles.
Jagged ice hangs down to the ground
And the smooth but sharp ocean waves
Come crashing onto Antarctica's shore.

Short summers. Long winters, that's the way it goes,
The flat and steep land, the peaceful scenery,
But the noisy squawks and moans and groans of animals are there
And are going to stay.
Jagged and smooth, thick and thin, ice of all types.
But now global warming is affecting this.
The ice breaks off with a *crack!*
The squawk of penguins dies away
And the crash of the ocean fades to a ripple.

So let's protect Antarctica,
All of us, together
And it will stay for as long as we know it,
Forever and ever and ever.

Kate Lesenger (12)
Kelso High School, Kelso

Who Would Have Thought It Would End Up Like This?

Standing tall and proud
With my friends all around
A sea of green with the occasional burst of colour.
A truck came hurtling past me.
It made me jump and the birds flew a mile.
The truck was red with a man driving,
With an evil twinkle in his eye.
Hundreds of thousands of my friends on the back,
Stripped bare of their leaves and branches.

Day by day
My friends disappear.
More and more trucks leave satisfied.

The birds stopped singing.
The animals moved on.
There was no sign of life.
I was all alone.

Oh no, he's coming!
Evil look in his eye.
Chainsaw in hand.
Just last week I was happy.

I feel the slicing pain searing through me,
As I plunge to the ground.
My life flashes and I think, 'Did I have a purpose?'

Who would have thought it would end up like this?

Delli Woodhead (13)
Kelso High School, Kelso

Antarctica Poem

When I think of Antarctica,
I think of . . .

Waves crashing against the huge walls of glistening ice.
Round-bellied penguins, squawking loudly for their babies to come.
Helicopters humming overhead in the clear sky.
The wind, whistling eerily in the plain, vast valleys.

The colourful aurora up in the night sky.
Research stations, buzzing with clever scientists.
Huge glaciers, slowly falling from the mountains.
The large, still ocean, a sparkling blue.

Animal footprints imprinted in the snow.
High, crooked mountains surround the massive, cold landscape.
Smooth, clear ice sheets cover the ground.
Tall, thick icebergs tower high above the sea.

Big and small animals,
Waddling, walking or swimming.
Short summers, light all day,
Long winters, dark and grey.
Thick and thin ice, both clear and glistening.
Tall and short mountains, rough and jagged edges.

Global warming creeping up on us.
Melting the ice caps rapidly, without warning.
Tourists visiting and destroying this natural beauty.
Once warm and dry and known as Gondwana.

When I think of Antarctica.
I think of a vast, beautiful, ever-changing continent.

Amelia King (12)
Kelso High School, Kelso

Open Your Eyes

Close your eyes,
Imagine a world where nothing is green,
The sky is always grey with fumes,
Poisoned fish float on an oily sea,
People walk around in gas masks,
And smell of SPF 60
In a last attempt to avoid the sun's fatal rays.

Close your eyes
And the image improves,
The sky glows a healthy blue
And the grass radiates green,
People wander round smiling
Under the shade of leafy trees.

Open your eyes,
Where would you rather be?
Remember that next time
You leave the tap on, or the TV on standby.
Where would you rather be?

Hannah Girrity (14)
Kelso High School, Kelso

Antarctica

You think a lot of snow falls
But it's a fact that 6cm falls per year
All those penguins waddling
And the seals squabbling
Over 30,000 visitors each year
No one owns Antarctica
Because they have the Antarctica Treaty
Amazing, pure white icebergs
Floating gracefully in the freezing cold water
Coldest temperature ever recorded - 89.2°
Oh my that must be cold!

Rachael Horsburgh (12)
Kelso High School, Kelso

Antarctica

I walk along feeling and hearing the crunching of the snow.
I feel the chill on my cheeks.
I can just see in front of my eyes,
But then I see the southern lights,
Silver, blue, green, orange, yellow, red and much more.
The sunset shows the silhouettes of the penguins.
I'm resisting the temptation to just let go,
Because the wind is so strong.
Whilst the seals lie, the seabirds fly overhead.
As darkness falls it becomes bleak.
The sensationally strong smell of the salty sea is overwhelming.
I hear the waves crashing and eroding the ice shelves and cliffs.
The fish struggle for survival as the whales plunge at them.
I have given you a mental image of Antarctica,
This country is being destroyed due to us.
Even though we are the other side of the world.
We are destroying one of the most beautiful continents
And we are making it become threatened.
So we have to stop!

Mark McCarry (12)
Kelso High School, Kelso

Antarctica Poem

A s the penguins swim through the ice blue waters,
N ever stopping to take a look at the mountainous landscape,
T rying to feed on the colourful fish below.
A mid the snow-mass on the land nearby
R acing petrels fly up high.
C limate change threatening environment.
T idal waves lapping over the mother seal and her pups.
I n the sub-zero seas she teaches them to swim.
C ruise ship on the horizon with tourists on board,
A ll hoping to get a glimpse of this natural paradise.

Sophie Douglas (12)
Kelso High School, Kelso

Natural Antarctic

Though Antarctica may be far away
we change it slightly day by day.
its pure, crisp ice melts rapidly,
its pristine atmosphere is gradually being spoilt
by our modern ways.

Recycling restores its clean environment,
the refreshing, salty smell of the southern ocean,
the natural chill in the Antarctic air.
Reusing items can help keep things the same.
The bleak landscaping is under threat
because of our waste and misuse of electricity.

By pressing the off button,
rather than the standby button,
we can save an innocent penguin or a baby seal.

Protecting Antarctica and its undeveloped atmosphere
will have various rewards for various continents.
Standing, staring into a colony of colours,
red, pink, orange and yellow, blending in the sunset,
all is peaceful apart from the splashing of the waves
and the quiet sound of a glacier creaking.
In a few decades, if we continue the way we are,
it will be almost impossible to experience this.
Keep it *natural!*

Melissa Dunkley (12)
Kelso High School, Kelso

Antarctica - An Icy Hell

Antarctica is a snowy place,
Devoid of most of the human race.
Smells like snow, tastes like ice,
View is white and not too nice.
Can't touch concrete, can't hear cars,
The best things in life, Antarctica bars.

Matthew Innes (13)
Kelso High School, Kelso

Antarctica

With its amazing landscape
And icy sea,
There's no other place its wildlife would rather be.
Penguins, seals and the Arctic fox,
Glaciers, blizzards and mountainous rocks.

With temperatures as low as minus 50 degrees,
It's a hard place for people, plants and trees.
Antarctica is an untouched place,
With its clean air, it's ideal for studying space.

The aurora is a wonderful sight,
Especially from April with four months of light.
There is eighty percent of the world's water there,
It's about time more people started to care.

Kyla Hogg (13)
Kelso High School, Kelso

A Taste Of Antarctica

I can see some penguins,
The feathers black as coal.
I can hear the ice,
Cracking like one thousand whips.
I can smell the fresh air,
So cold, it hurts to breathe.
I can taste the sea's spray,
Salty in my mouth.
I can feel the snow,
Falling to the ground like feathers.
We should think about Antarctica
And all its beautiful features.
We should try and help it survive,
By saving energy and water.
Please don't ruin this beautiful continent,
Save it instead!

Molly Hogg (12)
Kelso High School, Kelso

Antarctica - A Melting Continent

The landscape there is water and ice,
No tourists allowed, to keep the place nice,
Waste's so white, like a clean, polished floor,
Wind and cold behind the door.
Not much there has been seen,
Ice waiting, polished and gleam.
No native people can live there,
With the wind and cold in the air.
Last true wild place,
Nobody owns it, there is a bidding race.
No country really wants it,
Have to keep the place fed, watered and lit.
All its got is ice and an ice drilling kit,
Wanting to know what's living below.
Dinosaurs, aliens, UFOs, nobody knows.
Penguins are the guards of this land,
It is their job, it remains unmanned.
This sacred place is breaking up,
Truth? Lie? Making it up?

Oran MacKechnie (12)
Kelso High School, Kelso

Antarctica

A ntarctica has problems and pluses,
N ever-ending ice and snow covering the continent
T oo much pollution coming from us
A eroplanes fly in, with scientists on board
R esearch is constant, about space and life
C lever animals, penguins and seals
T oo beautiful at times, the colours in the sky
I ndigo and violet, blue and white
C an you feel the freshest air, taste the salty sea?
A ntarctica has problems and pluses,
    But its beauty is indescribable.

Matt Laidler (12)
Kelso High School, Kelso

Will They Think The Same?

When I think of Antarctica
I think of cute penguins
And white ice.

When I think of Antarctica
I think of whales
And free land for miles.

When I think of Antarctica
I think of seals
And clean, fresh air.

When I think of Antarctica
I think of beautiful landscapes
And the last unspoilt place on Earth.

But when all our kids and grandkids think of Antarctica
Will they think the same?
Hopefully they will
But with your help they have more chance.

Zoe Reid (12)
Kelso High School, Kelso

Protecting Antarctica

It's under threat,
But why is it?
Because of us,
We have polluted it,
Destroyed it.
All we need to do is
Recycle, this will help.
Don't take the car,
Walk if possible.
Soon it will affect us.

Duncan Rennie (13)
Kelso High School, Kelso

The Cure Is Disappearing

Home to thousands of living species
More colour than a paint shop
Noisier than a crowded football pitch
Disappearing like ice in a roasting desert
The beautiful rainforest.

Many secrets are hidden like a needle in a haystack
But they will never be discovered
Animals will be extinct being found
The weird and wonderful flowers
Hidden amongst trees and greenery
Could hold the cure for cancer
But this will never be found
If we let deforestation continue.

Do you want to be the one suffering from cancer?
The cure is further away from being found.
Every time a tree is cut down in the rainforest
Think cure, think stop deforestation.

Gillian Forsyth (14)
Kelso High School, Kelso

Antarctica

A nimals are in danger because of pollution
N othing there but ice and cold
T he ice is so fresh, clear and smooth
A ntarctica's sunset is so red and inspiring
R eally warm clothing is needed
C old and never warm
T he environment needs protecting
I see the penguins waddle around catching fish
C reaking glaciers move very slowly
A ntarctica is a cool place!

Ellie Bennett (13)
Kelso High School, Kelso

Oh Antarctica

The clear sky,
The freezing cold snow,
The plants in Antarctica
That love to grow.

The beautiful scent,
The mountains so high,
The birds that don't like this,
They say bye-bye.

The outstanding view,
The empty space,
The freezing cold air,
That shivers your face.

The sunset so colourful,
The really dark sky,
Oh, I love the trees that grow
Really high.

The splashes on the water,
The sparkling ice,
The feel of the snow,
That feels so nice.

The noise of the animals,
The salt in the sea,
Oh Antarctica,
How beautiful you can be!

Emma Younger (13)
Kelso High School, Kelso

Icy Antarctica

Snow falls, wind blows,
Then you realise you have lost your toes.
A chunk of ice breaks away,
Then you know you will have to pay.

Ryan Paterson (12)
Kelso High School, Kelso

Acting Now

Climate change is very bad
Climate change is very sad
Climate change is upsetting
Climate change can be life threatening

Weather is more unpredictable
Natural disasters taking place more with hurricanes and tsunamis
Ice is melting, causing the seas to rise
Temperatures changing are destroying the coral reefs

Climate change is resulting in
Winter sports dying out in Scotland
Fish dying because the water is the wrong temperature
Smog covers beautiful cities

Floods are wiping out animal and human homes
Forest fires are damaging large areas of forest
This is all very upsetting
This is all very disappointing

The red is of blood and fire
The blue is of floods and cold
The green of the wild is turning brown
The blue of the world is turning black

We can do something about this
It is now time to stop talking
And start acting
We can make a difference now.

Ewan Travers (14)
Kelso High School, Kelso

Cold Antarctica

Wind is blowing, it's stormy weather
Snow is falling as light as a feather
Penguins dip and fishes dive
There are only a few seals that are still alive.

Josh Osbourne (13)
Kelso High School, Kelso

My Favourite Place

It was the best place I knew . . .
You could taste the freshness in the air,
At night the beautiful aurora shone down from the heavens.
The proud seal's cries could be heard for miles,
But, then it changed,
The humans got greedy and started polluting the best place on Earth.

The animals found it hard to survive,
A once pristine environment was falling into deterioration.

I wish it was still the same,
Bitter but beautiful, salty but sweet.
If we all work together we can change it back,
But we have to start now.

Keith Fingland (13)
Kelso High School, Kelso

Desert

A desert of smooth, deep, velvet snow.
Untouched by man forever.
A harsh cacophony of piercing silence
Ringing in your ears.
A concertina of ice, played by giants in the sky,
Crashes to the sea, to melt and slowly die.
The land is drowning, the sand is gone.
The shells are on the beach no more,
For the fields and the roads, the paths and the towns
Are the rising sea's new floor.
A desert of smooth, deep, velvet snow,
Untouched by man no more.

Beth Hadshar (12)
Kelso High School, Kelso

Cracking

Global warming is a deadly foe,
Melting the ice caps as they go,
The ice caves are going from high to low,
The shelf is cracking . . . cracking . . . cracking

The shelf is hanging by a thread,
Dripping daily, as heavy as lead,
Antarctica's animals will be dead,
The shelf is cracking . . . cracking . . . cracking

The solution is up to you and me,
Let us prove it's not a myth,
Antarctica's melting can't you see?
The shelf is cracking . . . cracking . . . cracking.

Cameron Smith (12)
Kelso High School, Kelso

Antarctica's Storm

Ice everywhere and in every form,
Antarctica's getting ready for a freezing storm.
Penguins huddle,
Conserving heat,
Before they're covered
In a snowy sheet.
Scientists are aware,
So they prepare,
For temperatures below minus 50 degrees
As the wind blows
The sky snows
And suddenly . . . Antarctica froze.

Erin Hastie (13)
Kelso High School, Kelso

Ode To Antarctica

A cold blast of clean, pure air smacks me in the face as I walk
    across the ice.
N o tribes, no colonies or towns for as far as the eye can see.
T he howling wind, the creaking ice, the feathery snowflakes,
    they all surround an otherwise empty land.
A nimals swimming, animals hunting, animals being hunted,
    they all play an essential part in one thing - *survival.*
R ivers of ice, slowly moving towards the sea like a drop of ice cream
    slowly moving down the side of a cone.
C ruel Mother Nature takes her toll on Antarctica and could one day
    destroy the ice caps.
T he thought of ice caps melting, the thought of all the animals dying,
    the thought of sea levels rising and losing fresh water.
    It all empowers me with a feeling of responsibility and the power
    to do something about it.
I ce shelves hanging on by no more than a single thread.
C ould all the pollution we cause be the end for the cute, little
    penguins, think about it, you can make a difference.
A ll these things I have said about Antarctica just make me want
    to change its future.
    Will you help me?

Ian Peter Reed (13)
Kelso High School, Kelso

Cold

Antarctica
Not warm then
Too cold for a barbecue
Animals and extinction
Respect for the way it is
Too cold for lions and elephants
It's got altitude and attitude
Coldest temperature is -89° - you would need a big scarf!
All year darkness except for summer.

Cecily Withall (12)
Kelso High School, Kelso

Life On The Street

Walking down the crowded, dirty street,
Filled with empty, nameless faces.
Having not a care in the world,
You casually glance down to your right,
There you see a cold, desperate young face,
Looking up at you, pleading with you to help.
They're sat there, hour after hour, waiting,
Waiting for someone to help them.
Each time they catch someone's eye
They carry on as normal, chatting on their phone,
Disappointment enters their souls,
After all the days of this, they haven't become immune.

You toil with yourself, in your head,
Why choose to help this desperate person?
When in just a few seconds you'll meet another one.
You know you can't help this person, somebody else will.
Personal argument over, you gently, slowly reach inside your purse,
Throwing a £2 coin into their old, battered bonnet,
A grateful face looks up at you, overjoyed with your contribution.
You get a sense of purpose and happiness,
Knowing that in a small way
You have helped the world seem a better place.

Sarah Gibson (15)
Kelso High School, Kelso

Save Antarctica

Over one thousand miles away lies Antarctica.
As my visit started to Antarctica
I could hear the wind whistling
as I was walking through the soft, fresh snow.
it's huge,
it's big,
it's covered in ice.
So please save Antarctica.

Michael Berrett (12)
Kelso High School, Kelso

Antarctic Help

A ll the ice is melting
N othing will be spared
T ime to act
A nd save the planet
R ubbish to be recycled
C lean the planet's air
T his is what I'm talking about
I t must happen everywhere
C all in the parliament
A ntarctic action is now here.

Rory Connochie (12)
Kelso High School, Kelso

Antarctica

A ntarctica, looking so bare
N obody living there
T ake a walk, I dare
A ll the snow and ice
R olling on and on, so nice
C old and wet, never fret
T ake care to wrap up warm
I cebergs standing so tall and white
C old, you stand and gaze
A ntarctica, you'll never forget.

Eilidh Mathewson (12)
Kelso High School, Kelso

Antarctica Specialities

A s cold as ice
N ot spoiled
T oo pure for everyone
A s precious as diamonds
R eally helpful
C alm and peaceful
T oo cool for school
I nexplicable beauty
C razily special
A bsolutely unique.

Levi Hill (12)
Kelso High School, Kelso

Antarctica

A mazingly cold
N ow under threat
T ime is running out to save it
A n amazing, white continent
R ocky and mountainous
C lear skies are rare in winter
T he sea is freezing
I nspiring and beautiful
C overed in ice and snow
A nimals are running out.

Kyle David Walker (12)
Kelso High School, Kelso

Antarctica

White and clean
Untouched and clear
Nobody lives there

Massive in size
Bigger than America
Absolutely huge

Bitterly cold
Freezes your breath
Makes water turn to ice

Seals grunting
Birds screeching
Whales singing

Oil slicks in the sea
Minerals mined
Litter everywhere

Recycle here
Reuse here
Protect there.

Benjamin Hawkin (12)
Kelso High School, Kelso

Antarctica

Four times bigger than the USA.
There are no permanent residents.
Temperatures often fall to -50°.
4000m deep the ice can go.
Most wildlife lives in the sea,
With winds blowing at 190mph.
Antarctica was first imagined
By the ancient Greeks,
But never seen until 1820.

Aynsley Douglas (12)
Kelso High School, Kelso

Endangered Animals

Animals are dying
because of us.
We poach them for
fur, tusks and bones.
Cutting down trees and
shelters where they
hide.
Killing their food source.

Climate change which
some animals cannot
cope with.
Animals may only be
seen in zoos if
we don't do something
to help them.

Rachel Macvicar (13)
Kelso High School, Kelso

Antarctica

A mazing experience but not dangerous
N ice
T errific sights
A nimals are seen all over the place
R eally cool glaciers
C old all the time
T orturous weather
I cebergs are amazing
C reatures like krill and plankton
A ntarctica is the best!

Cameron Bryce (12)
Kelso High School, Kelso

Isn't It Sad?

Isn't it sad to see the old woman
Sitting outside the rundown factory?
Cold, damp, hungry and alone.

Isn't is sad to see young families
Homeless and literally starving,
Working for practically nothing?

Isn't it sad to see cities being bombed?
Millions upon millions of people dying for no reason.

Isn't it sad to live in a world
Full of anger and conflict,
A world of poverty and war?

We *can* make a difference.

Megan Cuthers (14)
Kelso High School, Kelso

Antarctica

A ltitude - world record
N ear enough the most popular animal is a penguin
T he Antarctica Treaty means no one owns it
A mazing white icebergs
R unning through the snow my feet are going to fall off
C oldest place in the world
T rees, never seen in Antarctica
I ce, ice covers most of Antarctica
C old, cold, coldest temperature - -89.2°C
A ntarctica, the windiest place.

Lucy Pringle (12)
Kelso High School, Kelso

Save Our Planet

S upport environmental charities
A lways try to reuse
V anish pollution
E ndangered species

O rganise money raising events
U nite the world
R enewable energy

P lant trees
L arge solar panels
A lways recycle
N otify others
E nergy saving light bulbs
T ry to reduce waste.

Daniella Pannone (14)
Kelso High School, Kelso

Antarctica

A mazing place
N othing but ice
T owering mountains
A lonely desert
R ocky rocks
C hilly place
T ourists love to go there
I ce is all you can see
C oldest continent
A nimals everywhere.

Brittany Barnes (12)
Kelso High School, Kelso

Can We Really Make A Difference?

Can we really make a difference?
Stop endangered species becoming extinct?
Stop climate change or the greenhouse effect?
Stop our planet being polluted?
Stop the deforestation of rainforests?
Can we really make a difference?

If we work together we could try.
We should conserve what we have, before it is too late.
We should save energy, not leave appliances on standby.
We should reduce our CO_2 emissions by using public transport.
We should recycle instead of wasting new materials.
If we work together we could try.

Can we really make a difference?
If we work together we could try.

Heather Georgina Portsmouth (15)
Kelso High School, Kelso

Recycling

Instead of throwing things away
Just think a moment and see what you say
Don't throw away plastic bottles and cans in the bin
Recycling would be the thing.

Tall, black, wheelie bins in the street
Full of packaging from the food we eat
Don't throw paper in the bin
Recycling would be the thing.

Lots of cut up twigs and grass
Along with all the smashed up glass
Don't throw garden rubbish in the bin
Recycling would be the thing.

Kirsty Hill (15)
Kelso High School, Kelso

Antarctica

Antarctica,
A world of cold,
A world of blizzards,
A world with some unknown,
A world with snow and sea,
Someone's land it never can be.
Years ago no people went there,
No rubbish, no fumes to fill the air.
Now is now and then was then,
And we have been polluting it again and again.

Global warming is melting its ice,
Soon we'll be thinking, *why didn't we treat the Earth right?*
Antarctica wants to be left alone,
To show its beauty and unknown.
A world of blizzards,
A world with creatures,
A world that goes on for thousands of metres.

leeke Green-Roberts (12)
Kelso High School, Kelso

Our Planet

Destruction of the rainforest, cutting down of trees,
The rising depth of the world's seas.
Many carrier bags adding to pollution,
Are bio-degradable bags the solution?
Destruction of habitats for penguins and polar bears,
You would have thought more people would care.
The whole planet could try to recycle,
Even if it's only old parts of a rusty bicycle.
Melting ice caps,
Reducing the land on world maps.
So let's try to keep the world clean
And keep the whole planet green!

Rachael Deans (14)
Kelso High School, Kelso

Let Us Begin

Stop feeding your avaricious fires with coal,
And maybe Earth's children won't inhale your fumes,
Maybe city air will be safe to swallow.

Stop discarding material as though it has only one use
And maybe plastic bags won't sail down rivers,
Or frolic mischievously in the branches of trees.

Stop throwing away your cuisine and your aliment
As though there aren't a million starving people in the world,
Then maybe, one day, each one of them can sit down to a meal.

Stop selfishly slashing down our forests,
As if we do not need to respire.
As though you think there's already a cure for every disease.

Stop ridding our continents of innocent creatures,
As it they have the ability to protest against their finish,
Lower your weapons, you must speak out for them.

Stop thoughtlessly dropping your litter,
As if other people won't have to walk in your filth,
Then maybe, empty cans and wrappers won't decorate our streets.

I inform you this is the twenty-first century,
So tell me now if you are guilty,
Is it not our duty to stand up against what is wrong?

The future's on you, think about it.

Apithanny Bourne (14)
Kelso High School, Kelso

Before

The grass is grey
Now.
It was once green,
Before . . .
Before we thoughtlessly destroyed the rainforests
Before every second, animals were nearly extinct
Before our climate was changed beyond recognition
People used to smile.
Before there were children too dehydrated for tears
Before knives and guns ruled the streets
Before suicides and killing were regular occurrences
Before drugs were readily available
There once was hope.

Before slavery
Before smoke filled skies
Sheltered the homeless.

Before people thought £1 per week was fair pay
Before there was racism and war
Before people were reduced to fighting over grain
Just stop and think.

This is the only planet we have
And at this rate,
It will never be green again.

Patricia Fingland (14)
Kelso High School, Kelso

Is This Right?

I see
black, smoke, litter.

We are killing our planet.
The air is filled with CO_2
due to the cars we insist on using.
The rivers are no longer clean.
Too lazy to go to a recycling park, so we dump it.

Is this right?

Why can't the black turn to green?
The smoke to fresh air?
The litter disappear?
Will I ever breathe fresh air?
Shouldn't we walk and recycle more?
Turn off what we aren't using?
Make the effort to recycle
rather than dump it?

Is this right?

it's not just you
that needs to change,
it's *everyone!*

Make that change,
Make that effort,
Or this planet and everything on it
Will die.

Is this right?

Chelsea Blyth (13)
Kelso High School, Kelso

Chernobyl Disaster

A red necklace
My ironic scar,
My Belarussian treasure
A rare jewel, cruel and raw,
The illegitimate child
By an accidental disaster
An accidental loss.
Venturing into a nuclear abyss
A cavern of unknown power
A fatal experiment
They could not outrun their own mistake
They had no place to hide
For the tragedy seeped through the city
Merciless to its creator.

They wept for themselves
For their families
For poor strangers
Terrified
For us
And as they lay on their hospital beds
Condemned to our pitiless fate
They weep still, death their final apology.

A clean solution,
Turned into the dirt,
Lying lifeless
In Chernobyl's abandoned streets.
A tragedy that shattered nations
Marked eternally
On my throat.

Lucy Harding (14)
Kelso High School, Kelso

So Quiet, So Quiet

Quiet in the camp,
Quiet, until the gun fire starts.
You are rushed out of the camp,
You see the enemy on the top of a building with missiles.
They are pointed at your tanks.
Before you know it, the tank has exploded.
The thick, black smoke rushes to the sky,
Like an eagle about to swoop down on its prey.
You rush to your jeep to get to the mounted gun,
Your partner starts up the engine,
You and your partner control the perimeter, shooting down enemies.
The ground troops sort out the enemy in the buildings.
After a few shots,
It's so quiet, so quiet.

Craig Andrew Riddell (13)
Kelso High School, Kelso

Antarctica

A ntarctica is the coldest place on Earth
N othing but ice, snow and sun
T he penguins are all squawking
A n unspoilt landscape
R are animals running around
C old air breezes along the land
T he ice is getting thinner
I ce covers most of the area
C limate change affects the ice
A ntarctica, the coldest place on Earth.

Liam Elliot (12)
Kelso High School, Kelso

Antarctica

Cold,
Cold and icy,
Cold and icy sits Antarctica, all alone.

Found by the sea,
Found by the sea animals,
always catching fish in the huge southern ocean.

Glaciers moving,
Glaciers moving, ever so slow
Glaciers moving ever so slow, Antarctica is full of snow.

Icicles rough and pointed,
Icicles rough and pointed, in the flat, abstract place.
Antarctica!

Stacey MacPherson (13)
Kelso High School, Kelso

Ode To Antarctica

A ntarctica, the last unspoiled place on Earth
N obody lives there at all
T he penguins are all sliding around
A ll the animals there are rare
R arely does anyone get to see it
C an anyone save the beautiful place
T he ice there is melting slowly away
I ce is all that surrounds you
C ars are making the ice melt
A ntarctica, the last unspoiled place on Earth.

Bruce Easton (13)
Kelso High School, Kelso

The World We Live In

S tarvation
A ids
V ictimisation
E thnic minorities

T errorism
H atred
E conomic unrest

W ar
O zone layer
R acism
L itter
D rought.

Kelly Younger (14)
Kelso High School, Kelso

Anatarctica

A nimals
N uclear
T emperature
A tmosphere
R ocks
C ontinent
T ransantarctic
I ce
C racking
A mundsen, Scott.

Graham Pike (12)
Kelso High School, Kelso

Littering The World

When you drop your rubbish
Do you know where it goes?
You may think someone picks it up,
But *ha,* that's not the case.
It gets washed down the drain
And round an animal's neck.
They will choke and they will gag,
With no one around to help them.
The animal may die
And there is nothing you can do,
Except, understand this;
You dropped rubbish instead of finding a bin,
Now that animal is dead,
And it's all your fault!

Amy Dodds (14)
Kelso High School, Kelso

Antarctica

It's cold
It's icy
It's always white
And very, very bright
With snow for evermore
You can see footprints on the floor
The ice-cold water
Never gets hotter
Because it's Antarctica.

Charlotte Gray (12)
Kelso High School, Kelso

All Over The World

All over the world there are bombs, killing.
There are soldiers firing guns.
People are raping and torturing and hurting,
Under our one burning sun.

All over the world there are children dying,
There is disease, starvation and dirt.
People are mourning and choking and screaming,
Consumed by their sadness and hurt.

But all over the world there are people singing!
There is joy and love and right!
People are learning and striving and hoping,
That we might one day reach the light.

Rose Hadshar (14)
Kelso High School, Kelso

Save The Rainforests

For all those fools out there
Who are cutting down the rainforests bare,
Think twice before you cut that tree,
Before I have to come and plea.
Because for every tree you chop down,
The world will eventually drown.
So think about those animals, the big and small,
Whose habitats seem to matter not at all.

So now a plea,
Try to make a difference for you and me!

James Stewart (14)
Kelso High School, Kelso

Go Green, Go Green, But What Does It Mean?

The world's in a frenzy,
A sudden panic,
Save the planet, save the planet.
Governments have gone manic,
Reduce, reuse, recycle they say,
It can be done every single day,
We must act now, anywhere, anyhow.

Cutting down is what we must do,
Conserve energy and fossil fuel too,
It's quite simple in actual fact,
To keep the atmosphere completely intact.

Go green, go green!
I know what it means!

Olivia Robson (14)
Kelso High School, Kelso

War

Boom! Bang! the sound of war.
Bodies lying everywhere.
Men screaming out.

The fields that were colourful and bright,
Now are grey and dull.
Thick with smoke,
The smell of death lurks around.

War is not a nice time,
It makes people feel depressed and alone,
Especially the ones who lose their family.

Marcus Wilson (13)
Kelso High School, Kelso

Antarctica

Antarctica

So old,
So cold.
Did you know
It's a desert of snow?
Blizzards of snow and lots of wind
Animals here cannot be skinned.

Splash, as icebergs hit the sea.
Animals in the water begin to flee.
Penguins stand in colonies,
Leopard seals wait in the seas.

Snow and ice stand big and tall,
But once in a while some bits fall.
Some bits rough and some bits smooth,
Lots of things here can begin to move.

Antarctica.

Sophie Fenwick (12)
Kelso High School, Kelso

Poaching

The elephants, in the wild, look peaceful,
They live in harmony with the land.
The poachers come with their guns and sick minds,
Filling the air with tensions and sorrow.

Shooting at anything that moves
And all for the elephant's tusks.
The bone that defends them.
It's murder,
Killing innocent animals for money and greed.
It has to stop.

Rachael Bennett (14)
Kelso High School, Kelso

Antarctica

The mountains stand tall,
Shielded with a crisp, white layer of snow.
The blue sky ripples slowly
And elegantly strides away,
Changing its cape to black.

Fireflies fly high, acting like stars
Filling the sky with light.
Icebergs glide silently on the cool, blue sea.

In the morning, when I wake up,
On the white sheet of snow
There are thousands of tracks made by tiny penguin feet.

Antarctica is cold,
Antarctica is icy,
Now it's time to leave,
This is such a crisis!

Briony Finlayson (12)
Kelso High School, Kelso

Does It Matter?

Playing for Scotland means a lot to anyone.
But just because you're black it shouldn't change anything.
It does!
If the home fans sing your name
And the away fans sing monkey chants at you,
Or throw things at you,
It hurts.

So let's switch colours and see
How you like it!

Liam Hill (13)
Kelso High School, Kelso

Antarctica

Antarctica hasn't got much colour,
With its howling blizzards and freezing temperatures,
Big or small ice blocks doesn't really matter,
They're all still dangerous like the glaciers.

There is no one around, peace and quiet,
Not trees rustling, just a penguin or two,
Fish swimming for hours and hours,
Beneath the ice-cold waters.

Abbie Hook (12)
Kelso High School, Kelso

Antarctica

A n amazing place
N obody owns it or lives there
T ourists love to go there
A nimals are its main inhabitants
R ocks in the dry valleys
C oldest continent ever
T reasures lie under the ice
I ce dominates this barren landscape
C ompletely flat in some places
A nd all this is being affected by global warming.

Holly Lowrie (13)
Kelso High School, Kelso

One Person

One person's idleness can fuel another's desire.
One person's ignorance sparks another person's fire.
One person's hatred is another person's love.
But if we all pull together we can reach the skies above.
The words are on our lips -
Save the World!

Natasha Gray (15)
Kelso High School, Kelso

Antarctica

Antarctica, like a lost ship surrounded by wild oceans,
All lonely, in the middle of nowhere,
The home of many innocent creatures,
Being destroyed by all those around it.
But what can we do to save these endangered lands?
Well, to start, you can put that energy-saving light bulb in place
And switch off that TV.
Picking up litter is just so easy,
So just take a moment to think
About this beautiful, pure place,
Because if you don't,
Well, it might just melt away.
Think!

Jack Bayram (13)
Kelso High School, Kelso

An Untouched Wonderland

The wind whips my face
Soft snow under my feet
Antarctica looks perfect
Untouched, all neat.

The penguins are squawking
They stand tall and proud
Antarctica's normally quiet
The penguins are loud.

Helping Antarctica can't be too hard
Are we just lazy? Or is it too far?
Still untouched, still safe
Please don't let this country go to waste.

Tessa Hunter (12)
Kelso High School, Kelso

Antarctica

A ngles, shapes of icicles dangling from penguin beaks,
N ot even a gram of 10 centigrade heat.
T emperature dropping far below fifty,
A ir becoming extremely grey and misty.
R ain tumbling down, freezing into ice,
C oming down from the heavens like puffed up grains of rice.
T ourists arriving in tiny, little planes,
I ndividual penguins sliding along quiet lanes.
C reamy white snow buzzing about in storms,
A lways making you miserable and feeling forlorn.

Rebecca Rogers (12)
Kelso High School, Kelso

Antarctica

A ntarctica is the coldest continent in the world
N uclear explosions are not allowed on this continent
T he coldest temperature recorded here was 89 degrees
A verage elevation level is 2,300 metres
R aging winds sweep across the continent
C rocodile ice fish are found here
T he opposite side of the world is the Arctic
I cebergs only show 10 percent above water level
C od fish are common on this continent
A ntarctica is known as the South Pole.

Emma Dunkley (12)
Kelso High School, Kelso

Antarctica

Antarctica, such a barren land,
Which nature only, does command.
Such a quiet, peaceful place.
Ruined by scientific waste.
Home to many, many things,
From fish with fins to birds with wings.
All the birds have lots of feathers,
To protect them from the weather.
And on this icy land,
Millions of huddled penguins stand.
While glaciers slide into the sea,
Mount Erebus glows silently.
In order for this beauty to last,
We must change our ways and fast!

Rebecca Mark (12)
Kelso High School, Kelso

Free Range

Free range chickens,
Free range grass,
Free range fruit,
Free range air,
Free range water,
Free range bears,
Free range cows,
Free range sheep.

Animals should have a free-range environment.

Shaun Sloggie (13)
Kilchuimen Academy, Fort Augustus

Hobo

The cold wind blows past my weary eyes,
And the box turns into ruins with the wind and snow,
My frozen fingers turning crippled and my knitted rugged
Gloves start burrowing in the snow.

The hobophobic people just walk past without a care,
They give me a glance in disgust and continue their journey.

My small empty cup in front of me still is . . .
Empty of money,
But full of pain and neglect.

People like us have feelings too,
But you believe we don't,
Maybe when you walk past the next time,
You might actually smile.

Tessa Campbell (12)
Kilchuimen Academy, Fort Augustus

Not Endangered, Or Are They?

They see in a way we never could,
They live in a place we never should,
They seem to be many as common as a penny.

They can really annoy but watch out, oh boy,
Within a few years, they all could be gone,
Extremely quickly like exploding a bomb.

They fly in the night; I think they're all right,
Some of them bite, some glide like a kite,
They can be big, they can be small,
I really love them all.

They can't all die - there's just no way,
Bats. They're not endangered . . .
Or are they?

David Saunders (12)
Kilchuimen Academy, Fort Augustus

Lone Wolf

Rumbles of the machines die away,
And they stay there for the night,
They had been working all day,
Giving an excuse for animals to run in fright.

One moon shines alone,
Though a million stars shine like eyes,
Across the land sails a sad tone,
As a lonely heart dies.

At the top of a meadow,
Howling a lonely tune,
Sits a hungry grey shadow,
Searching for the moon.

The wolf doesn't stop howling,
It howls all through the night,
Its stomach is growling,
It's looking for a fight.

Humans destroyed its food,
Humans destroyed its bed,
Humans don't care if they're rude,
And by morning the wolf lies dead.

Ella Lumsden (13)
Kilchuimen Academy, Fort Augustus

Night-Time Pollution!

Swamps of traffic,
Flashing of lights,
Buzz of tourists,
All through the night.

The pollution never stops,
The litter too,
I hope one day the pollution
Stops and it's true . . .

Jaclyn Emma Ross (13)
Kinlochbervie High School, Kinlochbervie

Dreadful Future

The grass is green,
The ocean's blue,
The land is fresh,
As if it was new.

But slowly moving,
Through the air,
Is a dreadful future,
That we won't bear.

The flowers bloom,
The deer graze,
But maybe this year,
Is the last of those days.

Smoke covers the world,
The sky is grey,
We did the damage,
And now we must pay.

Sophie MacLeod (12)
Kinlochbervie High School, Kinlochbervie

Homelessness!

Sitting on the streets,
Eating dog meats,
In a shop door,
Lying on the floor,
Living in a cardboard box,
Sleepin' with the town fox,
Wake up early,
Hair all curly,
He feels like nowt,
His life's up the spout,
Now he's *out!*

Ruairidh Forbes (13)
Kinlochbervie High School, Kinlochbervie

Why?

So many people starving to death,
Why?
When we are tucking into our grub,
Someone,
Somewhere,
Is choking to death,
On dirty water they walked miles to get,
Why?
When we work,
We get paid,
Why then do they get cheated?
The little food they could have used,
They were cheated out of,
Why?
Shouldn't someone do something?
So much money,
So little goes to them.
Why?

Erin Kish (12)
Kinlochbervie High School, Kinlochbervie

Litter

Lots of litter on the ground,
In the streets, more has been found,
Are people getting lazy,
Or is the message a bit hazy?
Pick it up, put it in the bin,
Then the animals can win,
Help save the planet,
Help the birds fly like a gannet.

Eilidh Clark (12)
Kinlochbervie High School, Kinlochbervie

Our Shame

This world, this wreck,
We are going up in flames,
The flames of our own ignorance.

World leaders think they can control,
This pollution at hand,
Pollution in the ground as well as in your back garden.

Smoke rising above the earth,
Like spires reaching into Heaven,
But even God is ashamed of what we have done,
And what we are doing.

Tom Robbins (12)
Kinlochbervie High School, Kinlochbervie

Hard Wood

Use soft wood,
Don't destroy the Amazon,
Lungs of the planet.

Mathew James Lenny Hathaway (12)
Kinlochbervie High School, Kinlochbervie

Big Blue Bin - Haiku

Recycle paper,
In the big, blue bin, open
Mouth and pop it in.

Gary Morrison (13)
Kinlochbervie High School, Kinlochbervie

Be Green

Pollution,
Litter,
These are some
Of the many things,
That are killing,
Our one change at survival.
Earth,
Life on this planet,
Is slowly draining,
Away so help now,
Not just you but everyone
Around us.
So if you do your part,
To keep our planet green,
So humans and animals,
Can stay on this planet,
For time to come,
Animals are becoming extinct,
The ozone layer,
Is being destroyed,
Who knows in just a few
Hundred years from now,
We could all be gone,
Forever!

Elizabeth Marsham (12)
Kinlochbervie High School, Kinlochbervie

Poverty

P oor people living in the deserts,
O ld people dying of diseases,
V ery small prices for the rice and cocoa beans grown,
E verywhere's so dry and so good crops aren't always grown,
R eally hungry but so little to eat,
T hirsty but with no clean water to drink,
Y can't everyone in the world be equal?

Charlie Craig (15)
Largs Academy, Largs

Homelessness

I sit and beg in the doorway,
All day, every day,
I sit there through rain, hail and fog,
Just me and my poor little dog.

They call me the 'tramp',
I can't even afford to send a letter with a stamp,
I have long greasy brown hair,
And no one at all seems to care.

I have never heard a good comment about me,
They all just say my dog has fleas,
I really, really, need something to eat,
I don't care if it's sweets, fish or meat.

No one gives me money because they expect me
                                    to spend it on drink,
I actually just want to stop the way I stink,
I am actually, really smelly,
I have nothing to do, because I can't afford a telly.

Stuart Rintoul (14)
Largs Academy, Largs

What Is The Point?

What is the point?
When the bangs are so loud,
They stop you from hearing,
When your friends fall beside you,
After losing all feeling.

When you're stuck in the mud,
Like a ship sinking down,
And your feet are near frozen,
Your fingertips also,
When you don't have the will,
To fight . . . to move on,
What is the point?

Ewen Brennan (15)
Largs Academy, Largs

I'm A Fat Racoon

I'm a racoon,
And I live on litter,
Stuff that people throw away,
Is my dinner,
It used to be quite hard,
For me to find some food,
But now I am totally fat,
Because the people are so good,
Their bins are overflowing,
Wrappers all over the ground,
Chocolate and crisps and other food,
That's what can be found,
I'm eating so much,
Except now I'm going to explode,
Help me go on a diet,
Help me lose a load of weight,
If you recycle stuff,
Instead of throwing everything away,
Then you'll save me from obesity,
And I'll live to eat another day.

Jenna Kirk (14)
Largs Academy, Largs

World War Life

Here I sit knee-deep in muck,
As bullets fly, we have to duck.
My brother sits next to me,
He's the only one left of three.
Trench-foot claims Kenny,
Bullets claim many.
Bang! That's Albert. *Bang!* That's Ray.
They go by the hundreds each day.
I am quite lucky I suppose,
But why this war? Nobody knows.

Claire Lennox (15)
Largs Academy, Largs

What A World

Not very fair,
Full of despair,
It is not too late,
To change our fate.
We need to be green,
To recycle, and help,
Protect the seashores and kelp,
Have less food miles,
To be able to see the smiles,
Of future generations,
In all the nations.
Let's not use the car,
Not travel so far,
To protect the ozone layer,
We each need to be a player,
To reduce our carbon footprint,
We *all* need to do our stint.

Laura Bonn (13)
Largs Academy, Largs

Just Me

She stood sadly in the rain,
Tears pouring down her face,
Nowhere to go,
Nothing to do.

She stood there in silence,
Thinking about the future,
Why does colour of skin matter?
Everyone is the same underneath,
So why was she standing there,
Cold and upset?
All thanks to racism.

Hannah Burns (14)
Largs Academy, Largs

This Is War

Bullets flying,
Infants crying,
People dying,
Governments lying,
Soldiers guarding,
Planes bombarding,
Armoured tanks and mines as warnings.

Snipers aiming,
Guerrillas maiming,
People praying,
Heroes saving,
Families breaking,
Knees are shaking,
History is in the making,
This is war.

Ruth McClelland (14)
Largs Academy, Largs

Silence

Desolation, desolation and death,
No winds or breezes,
Not a single breath.

No birds are singing,
No bells are ringing,
The guns are silent,
The men are quiet,
The air is thick with fear.

No planes are flying,
No medics are running,
The tanks have stopped,
No bombs are dropped.

And then the whistle blows . . .

Katy Johnstone (14)
Largs Academy, Largs

Black Power, White Power

Black power,
White power,
Between them both civilians cower,
But when the reaper comes to call,
At the end of it all,
It won't be your colour that matters,
A world divided,
The races collided,
Events in history help us remember,
The sheer evil of these racist pretenders,
Black power,
White power,
Between them both civilians cower.

Sam Hawker (13)
Largs Academy, Largs

Frightening Fighting

A shot from a gun,
In the middle of the night,
I wet myself,
And run in fright!
Bullets fly everywhere,
No wonder colonel's going spare,
Chaos! Panic! What the heck!
Everybody! Hit the deck!
People screaming,
Friend or foe?
Don't ask me,
How am I to know?
Bodies lying all around,
Can barely even see the ground,
Finally make it back to base,
It's guarded but we're still not safe.

Adam Murdoch (14)
Largs Academy, Largs

Young Writers - A World Of Difference Scotland

It Doesn't Matter

Black or white,
It doesn't matter,
We are all the same.

From India to Pakistan,
It doesn't matter,
We are all the same.

Jewish or Buddhist,
It doesn't mater,
We are all the same.

Catholic or Protestant,
It doesn't matter,
We are all the same.

Living or lived,
It doesn't matter,
We all die the same.

Lewis Smith (15)
Largs Academy, Largs

Why Me?

Just because,
The colour of my skin,
Just because,
I always let them win,
I can never keep my tears back,
Every time they call me black.
Why me? Just because the colour of my skin,
All the teachers say is,
Aw what a sin,
They don't care,
That everyone does stare,
Just because of the skin I wear.

William Seaton (15)
Largs Academy, Largs

The Dodo, Where'd It Go Go?

The dodo,
Where'd it go go?
Trapped by hunters,
Killed by poachers,
Taken by man to foreign countries,
Where they die of starvation,
Where are they in our nation?
Nowhere,
Gone forever,
While the world weeps . . .

Look at the tiger,
The largest of cats,
With fur the colour of gold,
And flashes of slick black,
Murdered for their skin as rugs,
On rich folks' floors,
Their beautiful faces
Used as coat hangers on doors.

Killed and stuffed to be shown in museums,
For the little kids to stare at for a second,
Then forgot about a minute later,
Is this what we want?

As well as the elephants,
Their glorious ivory tusks ripped out and sold,
To be keys on pianos, tables in homes,
Pointless objects which have other alternatives,
What are the next generation of children being taught?
That it's OK? 'Cause it's not.
There is only one question -
The dodo where'd it go go?

Katy Raeside (15)
Largs Academy, Largs

Lonely

He sits there come rain, hail wind or fog,
Just him, his raggy clothes and his faithfully scruffy dog,
His ice-cold hands clasp the *Big Issue* extremely tight,
All through the lonely day and the cold bitter nights,
The passing teenagers, take the mick, making him feel taunted,
As if his problems aren't enough, he knows he is
                                awkward and unwanted.

From his appearance he looks nothing more than
                                a tramp and a thief,
But he was once an intelligent man,
Who was destroyed by grief,
Although it is too late to save this man's life,
Who died alone without children, a home or a wife,
Homeless people can be helped to have a life too,
By hostels, charities and even you!

Faye Hynds (14)
Largs Academy, Largs

Peace, Man!

W hat the hell
A re we fighting for?
R etreat! Retreat! And it won't hurt at all!

H armony everywhere? Now just a childish dream!
A ll that's left is hatred and greed,
T oo many lives, lost and destroyed,
E veryone fighting, it's a dog-eat-dog world!

E very bit of hope, stamped on and torn!
V icious dictators, upon the poor scorn!
I s there hope of us living in harmony?
L ook what they've done, to my *childish* dream!

Lewis Thomson (13)
Largs Academy, Largs

Sounds Of The Jungle

As the sound of machines starts echoing,
Brrr, brrr, brrr,
I scatter under the branches of a tree,
All goes silent and another one gone,
1, 2, 3, 4, all my mates disappear,
I can now see a bright light,
The leaves covered once upon a time.

The time has come for the large walking
Vultures to come out,
Tick-tock, tick-tock,
Trampling the rainforest floor ever so slightly,
Sneakily, silently,
Creep, silence, creep, silence,
Bang another bird down,
Fluttering, floating down below.

Over the tops of the trees,
Slurp, slurp, slurp,
I glimpse the watering hole,
The large elephant sipping slow,
A silent dart takes him down,
Now for his tusks, the real poachers' prize,
Grind, grind, grind.

Furry critters scurry round,
Like a ball on a roulette board,
The hunter wearing his furry coat,
Tip, tap, tip, tap, tip, tap,
That's what my friends think,
Unaware, unknowing of the future,
To be skinned, scared, shocked and sad,
What will happen to me?

These days I find it hard,
To find every grub,
Like finding a needle in a haystack,
No food for me, no food for my friends,
This is the end of the winding road,
Like a wound on the skin,
Still time, still time, help me!
And my friends, I'm a dodo,
Bang! I'm dead!

Fiona A Clements (14)
Largs Academy, Largs

Poverty

I go to fetch the mucky water,
Carrying on my back, my two-year-old daughter,
All around me there are people crying,
Or even worse, young children dying.

We can't afford a roof, too high a price,
What's for tea tonight? Just more dry rice,
As I'm working in the field, the sun beating on my back,
I'm awaiting the day my death date's on the plaque.

Katherine Leigh Neilson (14)
Largs Academy, Largs

What Is The Point?

What is the point in all this fighting,
With all these innocent people getting treated like dirt?
How could someone have caused so much trouble,
And not care about all the pain and the hurt?

What is the point in causing so much fear,
Towards citizens who've done nothing wrong?
How can we not see the futility that exists?
We've been blind for far too long!

Sarah Jackson (14)
Largs Academy, Largs

Does Anyone Care?

Climate change,
Does anyone care?
The greenhouse gases occupying our air,
Climate change,
Does anyone know,
How long we've got till the rivers overflow?

The ozone layer,
The factory fumes,
That global warming,
Invading our news.

Climate change,
Does it really show?
Will oxygen levels reach an all time low?
Climate change,
It is happening here,
Should we conquer the problem or run in fear?

The icebergs melting,
The rivers rising,
High UV levels,
It's all so frightening.

Climate change,
What are we going to do?
Does anyone care?
It's happening here,
Your town, your city,
Does anyone care?
We can't see it,
But can we solve it?
Does anyone care?

Climate change,
Does anyone care?

Angela Flack (14)
Largs Academy, Largs

What Did I Do Wrong?

What is racism?
She thought about it to herself,
As she stood in the pouring rain,
Tears rolling down her face,
Is it because of the colour of my skin?
But why does that matter?
Everyone is the same!
What did I do wrong?

We all eat the same food,
Drink the same water,
Breathe the same air,
Why does all this happen?
What did I do wrong?
It's all thanks to racism!

Geraldine Murphy (14)
Largs Academy, Largs

The Ice Cube

I watch the ice,
Glistening in the sun,
Water trickles down the side,
Along the ground,
Sun still shining,
Beaming down,
I watch a puddle form,
As the ice disappears,
Vanishing, quickly . . .
Then it was gone.
Irreversible . . .
Within minutes,
The ice was gone,
Forever.

Jennifer Miller (14)
Largs Academy, Largs

Stop!

Racist faces,
People crying,
KKK and bombed up places.

Now it's here,
Let us fear,
Racism grows harder.

We must stop,
The hateful business,
For the good of our people,
Stop!

Euan Soutter (14)
Largs Academy, Largs

The Polar Bears

The burning sun is shining,
But the polar bears aren't dining,
They can't get to the seals,
So for them there's no lovely meals.

They are very, very sad,
As we have gone global warming,
We are trying so hard,
But the bears need some fatty lard.

The ice is melting,
The water is rising,
We are being flooded,
And the ice caps are capsizing.

We are destroying their homes,
And we are destroying ours,
If we don't make a change,
Then we'll end up living on Mars.

Connor Thomson (12)
Lornshill Academy, Alloa

Colours

Green, green,
Green as grass,
Green as green glass,
Green.

Blue, blue
Blue as the sky,
Blue as rivers running by,
Blue.

Brown, brown,
Brown as wood,
Brown as bird food,
Brown.

Yellow, yellow,
Yellow like the sun,
Yellow like butterflies having fun.

Colours, colours,
Green as trees,
Yellow as the honeybees,
Blue as rivers running by,
Brown as birds flying high.

Louise Hall (12)
Lornshill Academy, Alloa

Come On! Let's Save The Environment!

Step on that bus!
Forget about the car,
You're helping the environment,
A little bit does go far!

Walk to school,
Step by step, 1, 2, 3,
If you do this,
You might save a tree.

Turn off that light,
It's a simple thing to do,
We're saving the world,
Why don't you join us too?

Put your rubbish in the bin!
You don't need to drop it on the ground,
And at our school,
You might just win a pound.

So let's save the environment,
Everyone together,
Let's do our best,
And change the world forever.

Fiona Gillies (13)
Lornshill Academy, Alloa

Tiger

T ip-toeing through the forest,
I mprint is imperilled!
G reat groan, hunter near!
E dgy ears then echoed *roarrrr!*
R ed, red, red another creature dead!

Aneesa Burnside McCarthy (12)
Marr College, Troon

Tusks

Rough sandpaper skin,
Steadily treading along,
Terrifying tusks!

Floppy, flappy ears,
Stumpy body, heavy trunk,
Small, wrinkly eyes.

Cheerful, occupied,
Has not done anything wrong,
Slowly dying out.

In a flash of light,
They all attack, hell, riot,
Another one gone.

All for just two tusks,
A mess, a loss, tragedy,
Why all of the pain?

They should be ashamed,
The ivory industry,
Killing for money!

Callie Dorward (12)
Marr College, Troon

Tiger Tragedy

T iresome efforts to catch its prey,
I ntelligent, fearsome, runs away,
G unshots fired, hunters come,
E ndangered animals because of fur,
R un away, scared, found, dead.

Cameron Irvine (12)
Marr College, Troon

Panda Panic

The cuddly teddy bear sits,
Then starts to slowly climb a tree,
Sharp claws breaking away bark,
Scruffy white fur,
Black fur so soft,
And as black as soot,
Quietly they sit,
In their habitat,
Chewing on their bamboo,
All of a sudden they stop,
A noise,
Bang!
Crash!
They start, alarm!
An enemy,
Trees fall,
They run,
The forest habitat is being destroyed,
From a distance they watch in despair,
Whimpering,
Now there is not enough bamboo,
They are moving closer to being extinct.

Joanne Hannah (12)
Marr College, Troon

Elephants

E lephants, large and lovely with skin as rough as sandpaper,
L iving in the grassy lands of Africa and Asia,
E ndangered, slowly dying out!
P oached and harmed, chased for their tusks,
H orrible humans shooting them down,
A t the spill of blood, it's all over!
N o more left and no mothers with their calves,
T wo precious tusks like two lethal weapons,
S oon there will be none left!

Siobhan Rose (13)
Marr College, Troon

Seal!

In the shimmering deep blue sea,
Splashing out of the water,
Onto a near full beach.

When the hunters come to hunt, only some escape,
Hunters do it for a living taking creatures' skin,
Taking all prisoners.

Looking for their own food,
Becoming something else's food,
Soon gobbled by a shark.

Pollution poisons DNA,
Tangled up in fishing nets,
Being killed by our debris.

Liam Whitten (12)
Marr College, Troon

Chimpanzee

C ool as it protects its young,
H appy just now but, always on guard,
I mposters arrive and it's quick like a cheetah,
M achines in hands of bushmen hunters,
P repared for attack it is not,
A frican rainforests are harsh,
N o way out has the chimp,
Z oos will be homes to these poor chimps,
E verything is lost for them,
E ating is rare as food is scarce.

Cieron McDonald (12)
Marr College, Troon

Elephants

With their wrinkly skin and baggy eyes,
Elephants look like they are about to cry,
Their tusks grow at the age of two,
I would watch out, they could kill you.

There aren't many left because of poaching,
In the countries that are roasting,
They live in Africa, Asia and China,
People think the killings are minor.

Nobody deserves being treated like this,
Because their family and friends will really miss,
Their grey coloured pal,
Who should not be killed at all.

Nikki Smyth (13)
Marr College, Troon

A Panda's Life

Black 'n' white body, beautiful and cuddly,
Crawling along with its cubs.
A mother to some, a feared creature to others.
Another tree chopped, another panda drops.
Their habitat is crumbling, their stomachs are grumbling.

Louise Martin (12)
Marr College, Troon

Turtle

T here are only 10,000 left,
U nderneath the sea,
R ubbish bags are responsible for this,
T hey are dying out fast,
L etting them die will not help,
E xtinction will come unless we help them.

Matthew Reekie (12)
Marr College, Troon

Polar Bears

Enchanted white animals,
With cotton-like fur,
Big sharp claws and small stubby paws,
Feet like paddles,
Swimming in the sea,
Looking for their food,
Where can it be?

Chloe Dempster (12)
Marr College, Troon

Help Tackle Climate Change!

Even though baths may be preferred to showers,
More relaxing, bubbly and hotter,
Taking a shower instead of a bath,
Uses much less water.

Turning off lights when leaving the room,
May seem like pure simplicity,
But it's surprising how many people leave them on,
And waste valuable electricity.

Leaving the TV on standby,
Is another slip up people make,
But once polar bears die and winter disappears,
They'll regret such a simple mistake.

Turning the washing machine dial to 30,
May seem like a simple task,
But although it's basic, it helps save the world,
Is it really too much to ask?

None of these things that are asked of you,
Are anywhere out of your range,
So do your bit and help the world,
To tackle climate change!

Nicola Henderson (15)
Moffat Academy, Moffat

The Big Green Poetry Machine

The world today is twisted,
Violent, sick and wrong,
People are treated badly,
Just for being themselves.

A while ago in the news,
A gothic girl got beaten
By five or more teenage boys.
A week later she died.

How could people do this?
I'm about to tell you the truth.
The fact is that
People don't care.

Next thing there's air pollution,
We're killing Mother Earth.
We're wasting nature's gifts
Just for pleasure!

There is even racism and rapists
Roaming around the streets.
A racist insults your nationality
And a rapist forces love.

Even teenagers are involved,
They scare people to death.
Decent people can't go outside
Because of teenage gangs.

There are homeless Africans
Who have nothing
They would kill their family,
Just to have a home.

But there is something much worse,
A thing that everyone fears.
People lose their family
All because of *war!*

Why does it matter,
Just to prove you're right?
Why can't you get along,
Like before you began the war?

There is a way to stop this,
It's really quite simple,
All you have to do is . . .
Just don't do it!

I hope you start to realise
What's happening in the world,
I hope you feel what it's like
For everyone around you.

But unfortunately you don't care,
It's not happening to you
So why don't you just go away
And think about it . . . sorry.

Connor Brown
St Andrew's RC School, Kirkaldy

Things You Must Not Do

Use the wind to dry your hair,
Turn the TV off, use your mind,
Use stones to iron your clothes,
Use the bus or walk,
Read a book or walk the dog,
Do not get a flatscreen TV,
You can walk and recycle, people!

Imogen Samuel (8)
St Leonard's School, St Andrews

Memory - Haiku

Wind knocked the window,
Blue skies enveloped the world,
It's memory now.

On Kei Leong (14)
St Modan's High School, Stirling

Poverty!

We are the reason for poverty,
We've really made a mess,
But what do we do now,
Do we sort it or leave it?

Their houses, full of mud, germs and fleas,
But it's all they can afford,
These people are lucky to be here at all,
They can't afford food, they die in thousands.

While we sit, and think of spending money,
They are dreaming of having money,
And we are tucked up, happily, in bed,
While they are lying there dead.

The governments don't do anything,
They just sit back and look on,
As the world becomes poor.

Fraser McNair (13)
St Modan's High School, Stirling

Pollution Poem

P is for paper, floating in a river,
O is for oil, that runs into the sea,
L is for lumberjacks, tearing down trees,
L is for life, killed by the waste,
U is for us, and what we can do,
T is for time, which is running out,
I is for in danger, because the animals are dying,
O is for oxygen, that's dying with the trees,
N is for nothing, that is all that will be.

Ross Cunningham (13)
St Modan's High School, Stirling

Litter!

Litter, litter on the ground,
What can we do with what we've found?
Make new cars with cans and tins,
Instead of them wasting in old green bins,
Cloth, silk, card and paper,
Make them into something greater,
Save the planet, keep it green,
And in a hundred years,
It'll still be seen.

Stephen Lewis & Andrew MacDonald (13)
St Modan's High School, Stirling

The World

A timeless beauty,
That is being broken down,
By the cruel realities.

We'll make it nothing,
But a world long gone,
A dream, dead forever.

Lying discarded,
Once a jewel, now a stone,
All beauty is gone.

Erin Hamill (13)
St Modan's High School, Stirling

Waste - Haiku

The stench of the waste,
Flowing over the edge of
The forgotten world!

Gemma Miller (13)
St Modan's High School, Stirling

Tiny Tiger Cub

Tiny tiger cub,
Runs wild, free,
A sunbeam in the stripy grass,
Worriedly looking,
Lying on the ground,
Silent, not a sound,
Shots shatter the silence.

Emma McCormack (13)
St Modan's High School, Stirling

Land Of Forgotten Hope!

We have to escape this land,
We'll catch the boat just over the sand,
The gunshots are flying,
Millions of people are dying,
The medics just keep trying,
But hope is draining,
It feels like it's always raining,
It's too late I've been hit,
No more lights are being lit,
As I'm falling, falling, falling!

Lesley Wynne (14)
Stonelaw High School, Rutherglen

In The Street

If you see a poor man in the street,
Well don't just stand upon your feet,
Get on the ground,
Give him a pound,
Don't let him accept defeat.

Paul Kerr (13)
Stonelaw High School, Rutherglen

River Clyde

There once was a man from Burnside,
He polluted the big River Clyde,
Then one day,
He found a new way,
And recycled everything with pride.

Kate Fell (13)
Stonelaw High School, Rutherglen

The World

There once was a world clean and pure,
It would stay like that we were sure,
The world is now sad,
Cos we've made it bad,
Now all we want is a cure!

Jessica Richardson (13)
Stonelaw High School, Rutherglen

Environment

R ecycling helps the environment grow,
E nvironmental growth is key for survival,
C ycling to school cuts down on fuels,
Y es, we are all responsible for this,
C utting out waste will help us survive,
L iving like this keeps the world cleaner,
E co-friendly is how we should live.

Gareth Watt (12)
Strathallan School, Forgandenny

Plastic Bags

Plastic is fantastic,
Let me tell you why,
A lot of plastic can have a second use.

So why not give it a try,
Take it to the recycling place,
It can be given new life,
Could it be, if we all try hard, recycling could become rife.

But if we don't,
And we heat up faster,
Global warming,
Surely will cause disaster.

Rosie Williams (11)
Strathallan School, Forgandenny

Helping The Environment

It's bad that cars are giving off smoke,
But worse, people are thinking that it's a joke,
It's sad that no one wants to help,
Oh no! The sky is the colour of kelp (eww),
Big machines and cars and all,
Are not helping the environment, not at all!

Robyn Somerville (11)
Strathallan School, Forgandenny

Trees

There is no point in cutting down trees,
Because they give us oxygen,
Oxygen helps us live but the problem is that
Workers are cutting them down
To make materials so please do not cut them down,
Make them grow.

Monty Peeters (11)
Strathallan School, Forgandenny

A Warming World

In the Arctic far, far, away,
A chunk of ice fell off one day,
The chunk of ice fell in the sea,
As all the animals tried to flee.

Now day by day the ice begins to melt,
And all across the world the tremors are felt,
For now we know and need to change,
As our world starts to become strange.

Global warming has come to stay,
And now we are all going to pay,
But now we have only once chance,
Though some of us don't give a second glance,
Now endangered animals are going to die,
Because we thought global warming was a lie.

Now we look for a solution,
But it's simple just stop pollution!
An energy change is what we need,
But most power stations are powered by greed.

High above in the sky,
Greenhouse gases start to lie,
Now every day the animals cry,
As they know,
Plenty more people and animals will die.

Blair Watson (12)
Waid Academy, Anstruther

Poverty In The World

If I had one wish,
This is what I'd do,
I would wish for rain,
And a sea of blue.

If I could wish for anything,
This would be my wish,
Lots and lots of money,
And lots of fish.

If I was given something,
That never ends,
I'd wish for a happy life,
For everyone and their friends.

If I could have anything,
I'd wish it could be,
Crop for my mum and dad,
And a wonderful life for me.

If I had one wish,
I wish it could be,
Good clothes, food and water,
For my friends and family.

If I had one wish,
I'd wish for a school,
Filled with lots of teachers and pupils,
And a swimming pool!

If I could have anything,
This would be my request,
The world's life filled,
With the absolute best!

Lisa Allan (12)
Waid Academy, Anstruther

Young Writers Information

We hope you have enjoyed reading this book - and that you will continue to enjoy it in the coming years.

If you like reading and writing poetry drop us a line, or give us a call, and we'll send you a free information pack.

Alternatively if you would like to order further copies of this book or any of our other titles, then please give us a call or log onto our website at www.youngwriters.co.uk

**Young Writers Information
Remus House
Coltsfoot Drive
Woodston
Peterborough
PE2 9JX**

(01733) 890066